DEATH OF THE FIRST IDEA

DEATH OF THE FIRST IDEA

Poems

Rickey Laurentiis

 ALFRED A. KNOPF ✳ NEW YORK ✳ 2025

A BORZOI BOOK
FIRST HARDCOVER EDITION
PUBLISHED BY ALFRED A. KNOPF 2025

Published by Alfred A. Knopf, a division of Penguin Random House LLC, 1745 Broadway, New York, NY 10019.

Knopf, Borzoi Books, and the colophon are registered trademarks of Penguin Random House LLC.

LIBRARY OF CONGRESS CATALOGING-IN-PUBLICATION DATA
Names: Laurentiis, Rickey, author.
Title: Death of the first idea : poems / Rickey Laurentiis.
Description: First edition. | New York : Alfred A. Knopf, 2025.
Identifiers: LCCN 2024051112 (print) | LCCN 2024051113 (ebook) |
    ISBN 9780593802700 (hardcover) | ISBN 9780593802717 (ebook)
Subjects: LCGFT: Poetry.
Classification: LCC PS3612.A9442285 D43 2025 (print) |
    LCC PS3612.A9442285 (ebook) | DDC 811/.6—dc23/eng/20241108
LC record available at https://lccn.loc.gov/2024051112
LC ebook record available at https://lccn.loc.gov/2024051113

penguinrandomhouse.com | aaknopf.com

Printed in Canada
10 9 8 7 6 5 4 3 2 1

The authorized representative in the EU for product safety and compliance is Penguin Random House Ireland, Morrison Chambers, 32 Nassau Street, Dublin D02 YH68, Ireland, https://eu-contact.penguin.ie.

For Friendships lasting, especially yours,

Devan & Rachel Eliza—

Thank you.

And for my Families of McGhee, Cannon, Nero;

My Momma, Grandmother n'em.

I love you.

The Illuminative Way-Thru, Part Two of a Trilogy . . .

I shall not, therefore, be surprised if
some of the ancient responses required
a double, involved language, and obscurity.

—PLUTARCH, *ON THE PYTHIAN RESPONSES*

For who ever believed in the Ethiopians before actually seeing them?
or what is not deemed miraculous when first it comes into knowledge?
how many things are judged impossible before they actually occur?

—PLINY THE ELDER, *NATURAL HISTORY*, BOOK 7

Men are judge and party: so are women. Can an Angel be found?

—SIMONE DE BEAUVOIR, *THE SECOND SEX*

Contents

If your foot causes you to stumble, cut it off.

—JESUS OF NAZARETH, GOSPEL OF MATTHEW

DEATH OF THE FIRST IDEA

STEAL AWAY

—gyrovagi

Not to the Boy, not even *Quite* his Body, but to its Boundary,
I said, *You're what's wrong; now fall.* Was all I really wanted, really—
    Even conjured to say. For there are Rites some Holy Chosen Refuse be explained . . .

Day fell. The Day threw down, as she will, Hot remorses, and Rudely.
    Birds flew. Words convene New images between Old sounds. *Haunt me,*
Vaguely, Guide, now Haunt—my Voice speaking? But, hush, come welcome Mystery,
    no, Baby, let's steal away . . .

THE ARDENCY

—Which is why It was *before* the Body, preternatural, perfect
absorber, Singular, slowly pervading a Body, so the Soul is what I'll Know,
   Patient dreamer, deep still, Indigo, chaste with the Psyche's wings
All subliminal chiffon in two caches: one is Virtue, the other
   is Vice, like the Butterfly, both Values surprise as they flutter
the grieving air. *Yea!* that the sky is grieving such glory the Soul is,
   all glad Earth is harassed with its Beauty and scorched with its Force the more.

This is my Requiem for Beauty, Lord, a *Carmen* for the Lewdly Beautiful ones,
   who Care—a constant changeling practice, as like a sky: once, shy-born & Sweet, if a fierce
evident blue Loses its Boy-Sorry expression but is a sore character at Near twilight,
   Setting champagnely upon the Ground. Your gaze is a God's: it looks out, with offenses.
Or like the painted Red face of stepped Babylon; a Shrew; or like half Siren, all Shrewd, now,
   gone hither-&-yon, first see *Rattails* in the hair, now see *Silk,* unshorn curls
   gat this Phaethon, like some stupider Apollo, the Sun, two minutes confused yet vital on some
   Daresome ways.

Sun come down, in a Swagger, to smolt-Bright gold—that the sky be now fuchsia, *Farouche,*
   now Bubblegum, orange, Daffodils & Neon pinks, & lemon rinds: such Flashes an Action
painting up High as to make a feminine Scar of Beauty so prized it hurts. *It Hurts* . . . when it Mounts
   a Body—the Soul do—evident at life's crowning, here to bully that Craven ship, but yet Sublime,
which terrifies. (Behind the face, the Soul's a process.) But the God maketh our Face to *shine!*

IMPLICATIONS FOR AN ARRIVING MYSTICISM

I have no mother. I have no friend.
I have no father.

I have no lover. I have no mention.
I have no future.

I have no sister. I have no land.
I have no other.

I have no equal. I have no gypsum.
I have no ether.

I have no supper. I have no army.
I have not ransom enough.

I have no trust. I have no enemy
Because I have no friend.

Gods cannot sit equal
Among Man, where Man have fire

I gave them. I have no water
Left. I have no ground

Left. I have no sense, no image.
I have no sex

Left. Idea *urges*. I gave you all I
I could to much sensation, & thus

Justified my ways. Urges
Crept, only as star attends

The Dark diffusion. Slow
Obsession (*I choose to live*)

Burnt me to a Crisp.
Enclosed are ashes.

Yours—

2019

I could string him back up the tree, *Sir,* if you'd like.
     Return his skin's meaning to that easy distance, coal dust, blaze
And far-blacken him, Mr. William Brown. You
     Love how the blood muddies the Original,
The way it makes a stage of my speechifying, this leeching
     Capital almost from his dying,
Like an Activist. I know

I'm not supposed to sing

Of his ringing
     Penetrability, those holes I open impose *in*
On the form—but all I see is bullets, bullets discerning him,
     As years ago it was rope.
I could pull it tighter, finger each bullet deeper,
     If you'd like, an inch rougher,
Far enough to where becomes that second heat, erotic.

I could use the erotic,

Ma'am, if you'd like,
     So ungarish, baring not too frank
A mood, subtle so you need it.—*Funny*
     How some dark will move illicit if you close your eyes,
The way, say, my black
     Pleasure is named too explicit for a page, but this menace
I put in it is not.

I could yank and knot

The rope, if you'd like, him like a strange fragment
    In them trees,
And the word "again" spelled out his neck
    Would be the rope's predicate till let wild, patterned and
Fierce his moan.
    It is a tragedy. No. It is a sonnet: how I *know*
Already how he ends.

But I could make him

Her, if you'd like, regender them till merely
    Canvas for your "empathy,"
Soup for my mouth. Still, if I could *but* just get
    This blunt,
Burnt lynched body up
    From on
Out the pocket behind my eye

All trees could be themselves again, all sound.

COMMUNIQUÉ IN BRAIN (OR, *EARLY UNIVERSE*)

—before diagnosis

The voices came only very early
    only very early in my life in my life
they came they made a swell chorus
      made a swell chorus made a swell chorus
  crescendoing (*wing*) (*wing*) in my child life life life
I braced I relaxed and so they went they went
  away, now sirens

    *

      "I was walking down the street when I thought I saw
my mother looking at my mother she wasn't mother and that's
    when it all fell down," my aunt says (*she dead*) Rosemary in my head . . .

    *

  Present.
The Three Crazies toil, two paired wings going *fierceful, terrific,*
the last two wings strike *despair*

VISIBLE CITY

Washed in a green, webby light, festival, playing
A chord, playing the near-most exotique
For a sterner nation, a brass mirror, a song where the word

Sin stands out, is thought to, *Voudouisant,* anti-Puritan but not
anti-God, playing the flirt, saying you could land a landed kiss
Here, *quick, lick;* and,

Later, this City washed more literally and more blue
With waters as close as cousin Cuba, as far as the far-walked shores
Of a kindred Brazil,

So that it was its image, not just its people, not just our bodies puffy
As a hemorrhoid against the water's
Advancing image, that was flooded; and

If sense is true, insight like a deeper speech,
An art, if that is true, then it is between these many poles
The City is seen:

The city, not just the given
Notion of the City, that screen we call myth, call the dark,
But the brick and spit of it, iron, horseshit, the River,

A mosquito vetting its vein for blood, mud, August, the Cathedral
August, late Fall—it is in these, first, the Eyes build up significance,
Build toward old lines: New Orleans

As that Elusive text, seduce us, what is witnessed revised by the Light as radically
By its Waters, which is History, which means it'll slick *pass*
thru your very hands and ghost. You must cope the world.

BEAUTIFUL BOTTOM, BEAUTIFUL SHAME

The way he writhed
   Beneath the other man
Argued his loneliness,
   But he wasn't just a blank measure
Waiting to sound;
However much an O

His mouth made,
   He wasn't just an O—
Thrusting back, up,
   Against what is almost
Like a finger, tho
It isn't, always needing

To be touched
   Like a finger, to be held:
—I'm lonely.
   My waist cinched
Inward like some vintage
Japanese fan, the clever

Blade of my back,
   Working inch by inch
Toward a pleasure
   Half mine, the way fire
Pleases,
Wax pleases . . .

What does possession mean?
   No, really. Tell me.
That at this moment
   Someone beside myself can feel
How many times
I shudder?

Asked if I like it,
   I like it, I speak out
Those three syllables, mess myself.
   The point is, I think,
To empty—?
It feels good.

To be two men—two bodies?—
   Interlocked in a sentence
Still forming. We
   Danced the dance that says I want you,
Come closer,
Come in me.

No, really, he said
   As a whisper—Boy,
You want to be possessed.
   Because, you see, he'd been removed
From his body then,
Per usual,

His Beauty, like a talisman, offered,
His woundedness revealed—

DISAPPOINTMENT

I think writing thru my crisis as my crisis
During crisis, this

Disappointed me, where before I was 'fixed so high.
Black tourmaline. Now that I think

It don't matter what I think. The Tower,
The Fool. Doubt

Equipped me with a severe patience; doubt
Took over my mouth

And named convenience. If I rode brass horses
Thundering in my head,

I said nothing. If I said nothing,
Death. So a moon instead composed me.

Pearl. Haven't I disappointed
Everyone, Orisha, even the ants, look they desert me

With the repeal of my so-called genius?

A TRICKY SEMINAR

Forever here, Mister Dark, and tricking me,
Steaming from a manhole in America
Or else you're damp between the tense motions of the trees,
Revealing the breezy discourse of those trees, black
Sound. I can see now how everything
I've learned of you is wrong. How an air
Of dumb assumption lounged on my brow,
A liar, winking, claiming a shadow is as empty
As my childhood vision of the falling sun meant emptiness.
But every child knows what moves the wind at night,
Knows what leads some birds to develop their unrest
In the high green of some trees or, lower,
What leans against that tree's bark: a man? Or is it
The just-barely-intelligible idea of one? Head back,
Maybe eyes closed, moaning, working to his own hysteria
The erection rising like a haunted iron chain a ways from him.
If I move closer, carrying a glass cup? If my mouth
Be that cup? Tho I've known fear move as bravely
In this world, move like a physical man, it can *shoot* a boy—
So shoot me. Who said that? Voices again? Was it really
The black mandate of my tongue? But how could any breed
Of blackness ever wish, so to say, to be penetrated? I could tell you
How a foot in a handful of falling dust sounds
In the night, could tell the blood a mother cries
Once she feels that absence drop, like mercy, inside her,
But I cannot say what a bullet says as it enters a child's skin.
But come in. You can enter me, Mister Dark. Let
Tonight be the first night I deeper see the pregnant
Possibilities of your design. How your fingers move
To build such attitudes, turning a moaning of the wind
Into a man, making what is a tease of grass at the heel

Into terror, now pleasure, then back to grass again.
Aren't you the mirror in which all lights balance?
Aren't you the line on which all lines cross?
Anything lives in you, so that that dark over there
Can be the dark of Mr. Henry Dumas, Mr. Michael Brown,
still agents, fameless, & full of breath; that the dark
Right here can be the dark ground of my own bastard mind;
That this dark soul come closest to my lips Is a shadow's
knowledge, full & whelming, not ever empty,
Charitable as is wicked, risky as is good; fascination;
Perversion; and I move to it, to you, a shadow-chaser,
Hearing the birds make restlessness in the trees,
Watching the man stroke velvet from his body,
Head still back, maybe eyes parted, if he's singing now—
He's at that point when I must surrender
My knees to gravity, and, mouth ready, get-gone.
I'll choose what ground I lie on.

HYMN

—in the mirror

There's a Valley
A man's worked back makes
  And there's a violence, too
There's a River
  A man's low Voice makes
And is benevolence, too
  There's a Falcon
His fierce Attention makes
  And there's a violence, too
There's a way a man just
  Turns at you his Weight,
Crying, he, alone, *Am the One Hurt*
  Assumes malevolence, too
Turn Sudden color, Superior, repeating
  Scarlet, *I, solo, am hurt* so that violence
Turns the Spirals of a rising
  argument: *Wait! Listen*—
Yet his Violence chooses
  Not to hear but dismiss it, so that Choice,

Some choices, Shameless, random,
  Some evasions *seem* a violence, too—
Men choose the violences they deliver,
  like mirrors choose the subjects
of their Debt? Or is it by Accident? Look in,
  & what is it you think you see?
Yourself. Your Power. Your Prejudices
  come out the throat to take,
  like any Man, all the while, always
    The *nearest* man's side

or his Business or his Strident
    Evidence or Damage or any Benefit
of Doubt, his Wit, his Acumen
    And, of course, tho won't admit it,
Drum Violence, too, like I do?

Do I create Violence, too? Or call it Violation?
    What is it when I say *Yes* still mean
No? I say *No* but mean it.
    Is that a violence, too?
But—Offense, let it, degrees of Offense, hierarchies
    of Injury, declensions of Pain
Sat among *Violation, Vex,* and *Violences,* too

    Tho lately what I
I'm trying hard to Make Sense in me
    is Mad before is Meeker, less feral
yet is more *femme* than *feasible*
    and *Fine* yet *is* Upset, and *not* a man,

or Hardly was, so failed it sure,
    and sees no more the purpose for
the Value in the Claim.
    A man turns to you and names
Himself *the Emperor of Pain,*
    like it ain't possible
His tall Hubris hurt, & stridency hurt him first.
                       Why be a man

When there are Valleys you can be?
    Penetrate & you can glide them,
Take in their honest expanse
    As one better, second nature and see

Some shy ribbon of river move in tricky,
    patient wakes, the very
Line the Falcon takes
    Returning to the Falconer?
How be a Woman
    When her flight be wary, yet—

Is anyone Sovereign in that
    who-space contests before a Mirror,
As it chooses now to ground
    Eyes, down, surer, & in the self.
                        Cue: *Peace.*

I think it means that we
    can be some Other work
than we were Raised;
    That I can strike out *Him* for *Hymn*—
For singing up Benevolences, too
    For it's easy enough to conquer a Man
I look in his eyes, and grow 'pathetic' . . .

MUNDANE SONG

You go outside and the Trees don't know You're Black. The lilacs will chatter & break
  Themselves real bloom, real boon, whatever,
No matter your gender. You matter. You, 'Cross a Natural life, is who You is & makes
  briefest material, so you matter.
How we are Added unto, Candleheart, & taken from.
It matters. Your Afro may start matted now be combed to touch
The sky. Come up from the ground looking extra,
Extra fly, child, You include the Sky. You gape. You open
Your Blue mouth, and such the vulnerable universe falls out.

TOWARD A TALL LYRIC FOR PALESTINE
(OR, *SCRATCHING THE HARDER THINKING*)

2016, Palestine Festival of Literature

The native town is a crouching village, a town on its knees, a town wallowing in the mire. It is a town of niggers and dirty Arabs.

—FRANTZ FANON, *THE WRETCHED OF THE EARTH*

What doesn't resemble me is more beautiful.

—MAHMOUD DARWISH, "TO A YOUNG POET"

1.
Every a burning key expresses a subtle truth. Tell everything you've seen.

2.
Everything, recall, everything, regret, describe everything, admit everything, so you wake up, crying, to write a poem one day, late, telling everything you've seen.

3. JORDAN CROSSING
Where are you going? Say What is the business for where you are going? Give me your Passport. American, say your name. Why you say this *Black* American? What this mean, *you give a reading*? You are an author? You come here by yourself? Show me your book.

Spell your name. Have you any politics or recent activity that would concern Israel's citizens?

4.
Difficult in its own flame, a flame believes it must burn. *Palestine,* but said repeatedly, wants return.

5. JORDAN CROSSING
Where in America you were born? What again is your business? Who is your mother to you? Is your mother knowing you are here? Say the full name & location of your father—*you don't know?* Sit down, please. You will take & complete this form and wait, sit, for other security agent. Stand down.

6.

. . . It is not Possible, Sure . . . It is
not, all times, safe . . . It is not always
assured what you must come to know.
So everywhere Customs is dense with
anxiousness and so Still slouches,
terribly, further eastward, thru Qalandia
checkpoint, toward modest Jerusalem.

7.

To know, I think, I know. Walked
out of queue and every Arab in our
delegation also ordered out of queue to sit
down. Israel tells me wait. You must be
interrogated, deeply checked.

8. CHECKPOINT
See this, Traveler, is how one crosses
over?

9. CHECKPOINT
Traveler, *why* say *Black* American? Is
this you, here, getting denied?

10. BETHLEHEM
Beneath a Ceaseless Star, a
Consciousness is born. After watching the
Grown Man from Gaza crack into tears,
denied this singular Corridor into his own
country, Critique since is reborn.

11.

Fail distraction. But there, in the future,
in the Palestine I'm let in, where three
boys play under one open blue sky I get

distracted. Someone saying Don't collide
our Pains—

12.

Bethlehem is Aida Refugee Camp's
jagged impression on my Mind. Where
high cement found itself in debris, the
shocking visibility of Occupation urges.

13.

Still I did it. I made comparison.
Rudely rises the Blood for Solidarity?
Poignancy? Do I yearn for Justice to
come like the Sparrow. Let it. Now newer
knowledge breaks In, like, Let it.

14.

. . . Let *not.* But when I assumed a
Black Authority on suffering, that we
were top Winners of pain, I was an
insufferable fool. Then found out a
more distant, stranger, salty knowledge
approach.

15.

And I cried, real baby's breath.

16.

And I sensed a *Resonance* there.

17. REFUGEE CAMP
Soft-soft, a crying bouquet of tears,
walking with that privacy in mind, which
made a sort of film rove in my mind.
Something I could critique.

18.

So we will all be walked thru, led on
this hard, hard tour each given a burning
key. But a burning key insinuates a
burning door . . .

19.

I was overwhelmed by my crying,
thinking it took Right attention from the
place itself, the problem, the nuance, at
hand. So I think it was the details of a
blatant, *physical* Occupation disturbed.

20. ASTERISK

Privilege! made its crawl way to
describe me. Imagine that! To be some
doubler, multiple consciousness now or
ever, and on Sight. Some Palestinian
boys are playing . . .

21. SHADOW

. . . they were four very young, very
carefree, Boys who swing their joy like
hoops! To see the drama: a worn, random
Loveset-on-Wheels, a Sofa, they push
joyfully, like playing pilots! racecars!
They were with the Imagination, playing,
for a moment unavoidably just kids. Next
see that Wall's tall forestalling future loom
over them. So that who greeted them was
not me, per se, but a weird surrender.

22.

(*Baby's breath.*)

23.

. . . So it was an *AMERICAN* and
then *BLACK* privilege, splint me,
an experience, right then I *knew* I
experienced . . . ? Spoke none about
it. Made no poem, yet.

24. SPHINX

What key is the sad key?
What key is hot? What's the darkest
key to sound? What key raises alarm?

25.

No tears! Sentiment struck me soft,
and fair. Small panic struck me? to have
slurred histories? And Profundity I could
call the film behind my brow, irking up
guilt.

26.

. . . But is it my Voice, insisting the
Issue . . . Certain remarks, certain abject
Black premises . . . distract me
. . . what can I mean by deleting *of
warring, intifada, vapors mixed* from the
poem, elaborate with *Blood like Dew in
the Fields*?

27. THE WALL

Killings are thrilling, the Wall said,
and casual:

   (1) little infant trying,

   (2) women in their,

   (3) dogs sleeping,

   (4) boys?

28.

A Weird War on.

Is this true? The Birth of a nation
means always the Death of a former one?

29.

It means also, necessarily, another
Birth come forth in a World from World,
let Light from Light be Truth Reign over
us where we will have been Changed.

30. HOME

O let be *analogues* of light decorated
in that Future where I'm seated at a
corner-store bench outside Esplanade
mart. Sudden Ceaseless Star hung over
my spine is walking the City of a Few
Diasporas.

31. THE WALL

. . . where Borders are controlled,
every Checkpoint a cold, ribbed, caged
Conduit: Chattel turnstile, guarded by
artillery fire. This is what I saw.

32.

. . . So Israel is Herod? Or was this the
time Israel had no king. His gross power
coming as the Decider of who lives, dies,
is Refugee, and whether there is Right
of Return, Property, Sovereignty.

33. JERUSALEM

. . . But I felt a Cognizance I had felt
before. I was persuaded. Something
reeling across backlids' eyes, only one
Palestine, the Holy City, came Up with
Sudden Protest—

34. JERUSALEM SYNDROME

. . . Tears are cheap . . .

35.

. . . became stoic toward a barely
articulable pain, actually, explicitly,
stood separate and apart from my own
Imagination, of what up to then I had ever
Imagined, regarding old Violences.

36. LET SOLIDARITY BE

As if myself I could only see: that once
was true. As if myself could usually see
myself somewhere in pain's design: that
much is true. But in Palestine saw not
myself but something else, predicament &
shadow—

37.

And I saw it would be fine, this
solidarity. Saw that Simply *American*
describes a brat's Poverty of Attention;
or it booms Paternalism; or it greeds
easy Privileges and funds War, hideous
Exterminations, hideous Reasons, and
I was so confronted that I was one of
them, American.

38.

Or does Black Pain's History in
America, Powerlessness, and Pageantry
serve to rescue me from that American I
suddenly was? It was like I was culpable,
the one responsible, and an interrupted
Soul.

39.

Pain's terrific, exquisite arguments
for Absolute Attention tweets at a World
I heard somebody say definitively is
Anti-Black? Listen, Black people
have Hurt. Still, there I was somehow
the distance from the intimacy of the
thing . . .

40.

So my Soul found out it wasn't all alone
in pain. Right when Whiteness formed
the expensive shadow of a Boy called
White Phosphorus? called maybe *Reckless
Freedom*? called *Denied Re-entry, Water
Shortages, Stolen Homes, Gaza* . . . This is
what I saw.

41. CREOLE PASSING

but a Voice distracts us: "By Pine
Bluff," she say. "Arkansas, where they
make it," she say, speaking of such fog
as the White Phosphorus falling. Such
burning drawls, hardest to quit; the bones
taste it. "And it ships," she say, like too
lightly, "right down that Mississippi." Port
of Call, New Orleans.

42.

Yet to know it was my want to see
myself *as* that Phosphorus, at least to
be top Contender in its & the world's
injury, it became too gross. To *insist* that
that Blackerache I know is always in
The Available, it became, for a moment,
immature. To notice pessimism's sneaky
patterns over me, beginning to replace
my pain for all others like saying I was all
day broken and that I was all day sad, and
always tired so I *had* to make a change.

43.

The film again: Light slides across the
face of a body. Now beauty slides. Now
Dark does. But what key testifies claiming
possession? What key vandalizes the air?
Which key leads to Hellish knowledge or
Solomon's or Caesar's? What key loosed
to such discord such I knew that I'd let me
be changed.

44. CHECKPOINT

Is being Black to mean I'm so
consumed with the being Black? Our
next shot slams us back and is familiar:
rows of cotton dipped in historical red;
burnt cork; crows; rows of bullets ripped
into some resembling, slum skin, aching
Availability—

45. WITNESS

Out of Black plain again the grim
figures make an emergency, no—they
are simply soldiers I am seeing, Israeli,
and some of them Ethiopian; they
are soldiers carrying artillery fire I'm
seeing, the present tense and I shouldn't
sensationalize—

46.

This is my slop attempt at reportage,
message as it is, my *tall* ambition & what
I witnessed, what all I've been at labor to
say, respecting Power.

47. A BEGGAR RUNS AWAY

I never beg. But let's just say the
freedom of this poem *be* the chance of
its failure, which be the draw?

48. WITNESS

Bethlehem, where four boys are still
playing . . . "One can't enter a strong
person's house and take it by force
without tying his hands. Then loot his
house," the Gnostic said.

49. WITNESS

Jerusalem where Homes are Squatted
in by Birthrighters now Outright
repossessed by strangers holding
what feels wrong: Two Passports,
Two Homes—?

50. WITNESS

Hebron where Cemeteries soundly
Muslim given each headstone's slick
calligraphy leaning leftward are yet stones
being turned up disturbed by pleas for
Jewish bones.

51. WITNESS

Hebron again where I saw everything
I needed to see in the labored chainwork
of the overhanging canopy that keeps
rocks, heavy stones, from falling on the
shopkeepers' heads: took a video of the
Palestinian man who said, "Go back.
Tell it."

52. WITNESS

Haifa suddenly is lush green vertigo,
and suddenly the Mediterranean Sea,
when just the Wall's otherside is inclined
to desert. Before crossing, a civilian-
looking man comes aboard our bus with
rifle and makes us de-bus, be screened
again, be re-bused and driven in.

53.

Who wants a pacifying lyrical gospel
delivered knows by now I cannot please
them, that I am Culpable, that I have not
stopped this ego rolling down my cheeks
to give my witness.

54. HOME AGAIN WALKING

Unbelongedness turns us all out. When
I am home again, I will begin a change. I
will have walked half the city down from
whatever is its Egypt farther to Babylon
like giving oblation. My spine walking, I
will be perfect provocation, ancient gall.

55. TRUTH

I first saw myself as the shame I took,
fully, for myself, however many years
ago—But was written away from it.

56.

Admission is a later knowledge, I think.
And a Future's knowledge. And a slower
knowledge, I think to think.

57.

Freer worlds, I should always think, be
possible. I am persuaded. I saw it in the
still-for-singing beauty of the land, how
Ramallah makes a gold hum in my mouth,
rolling hills of my feet walked on frankly
and felt—

58. CHECKPOINT

—only a Resonance. What could it
urge me into songs again?

59. CHECKPOINT

How should I answer?

60. CHECKPOINT

What is given can be taken; what is
taken shall in the fields be replaced, but
who can return? Where are you going?
What is your business in going? Say, what
is your name?

61. CHECKPOINT

That I tried relate, in Palestine, to
Palestine; tried, versus Cure, to Care. *Let
there be among you you who understands.*
What is your country? What is your
Work? Say again, why you come here &
who knows? Call out the names.

62.

Everything, recall everything, regret,
describe everything; admit everything: so
you wake up, crying, to write a poem one
day, late, telling everything you've seen.

63.

Even a burning key expresses a subtle
truth. Tell everything you've seen.

IMPROVISING ON AN EARLY THEME (*OR, ONE COUNTRY*)

—age 26

I *wanted* to be released from it.
I *wanted* its impulses stunned to lead.
That body. Its breath.
Let it. Let the whole pageant
end. If my body had a river in it
I did drain it. If by the river
was a city, let a storm shock & drowned it.
When in the city was a boy made sick
from his body, the freak passions of it,
I letted him out—*his* brown skin
lifting two shells. Let it. Let all
his limbs be popped and unhinged. First
their penis, its quick flight, as if a comet.
The eight fingers next, then thumbs,
then tongue, till every star was on the floor,
dismissed, each pointed in its own
direction, each became a door
to the one country where *Her* body is
loved and made for.

TIRESIAD: THE PUNISHMENT OF TIRESIAS, I

Trading sex was ne'er a Woods's game for Two-Strung snakes,
so when he struck them She right then was Immediately Created a Woman.

—*See: Hesiod, Dikaiarchos, Klearchos, Ovid, Phlegon, et al.* . . .

COMING BACK TO POETRY (*OR, TRANS—?*)

I guess I've been androgynous (*in that ugly way*) all my days,
I didn't know. No one said *Know it.* But I mowed my green lawns well
ashamed: my buoyant, gay labor, like a crow flies, sweated for future. It made my Body swell
not at all, timid buddings no Roses & slowly; so I felt *insufficiently* male. So I craved, swell
Like ants in a colony, for more: "*Trans—?*" So the cheeky happiness made
   Like late mail, barely, carrying its special memos
Out to anyone, but few received. All my friendships; all my family, so
   half received me and I was like an anthill scattering. But what is so *Sexual* about wanting
     swell
scatter? Or different treatments? Or chores? that old Victorian *femme-only*
   Faint way I, no Female, could use Faint excusing me from lawn's hell?
No Heaven fell, but It was just Childish thinking; (*Unfair?*) Now I sit, crow-symbolic, still,
   thirty, Proto to a kind of Second Puberty, trapped, not yet in gender's manual traffic,
But in my own poem. This is progress. Just to be writing again any one poem.
   But I was saying something about fire—fire ants, rage?
   How they do their cryptic, patient work in spiraled pairings.

PRODIGY, VERSUS PRODIGY

Everywhere *elsewhere* menaces breathe.
　A Female *mater* gave birth to two babes, four heads,
So the River wept Vipers. Of the dual natures is a "half-male"
　Whisper among the commons & Greek slaves.
A one-year-old, born webbed, punishes an Archaic world,
　But, like Jews, live. By Haruspices, "must be atoned." Of the beauty
Of all Ethiopes, tallest among men, come men. Onyx. The Vultures fly;
　the Ibis; the Brazen Serpent on the Pole; the Vulture flies. Prodigy
Is meant as "bad omen" or "sick wonder"; "Freak" before it is a Modern
　"Child-Prodigy." When a child is born, stillborn, of an Egyptian male
"Catamite," it records, the *webby* "Vernix" of the child remains *in* its infinite
　Hood, like the Uncircumcised Penis. On Roman shores, Covenant.
Dark circles turn the sky. Care, the Uterus is a Fist. But by Roman eyes,
　Law, Comedy, if not by Blackest custom, a one-day-old, an *eight*-year-old,
A *ten*-year-old "Hermaphrodite" is seized & is ran to & is dashed
　(*Do you approve?*) waggish to the sea.

INTERIOR PANDEMIC TIME (*OR, BRONZE DISEASE*)

——2020

—But the Corrupted air is too Rude today.
Day Spell: *Et benedictus*
   fructus ventris tui, Iesus. Iesus is us, and he isn't,
any more than Byzantine raised halos and bronze
disease is us, and they are; so our Planet is locked down,
   Compelling grief.

FEELING MYSELF

—Nicki Minaj, ft. Beyoncé

1

So it's true that the Flesh
  (*must confess*)
Must tell & tell again how it hungers
  (*finna fess up*)
Been 'buked by, hit, hunted, scandalized . . .
  (*makes confession*)
And it Hurts to the dirt to hunger.

2

  But I see
That the Flesh it ain't just—
  Is not mere discourse "*of Flesh*"—
As it is a means toward
  That *toward* pressure:

 That Yearning-for (*Spur*)
(*Spoor*) the Kinds of Pleasure
  (*Pulse*) the Sense of Another
Palpable (*Crush*) Perceptible
  (*Orbits*) Nearby (*my body*)
Nearer (*makes flesh*) Nearest
  (*your body*) Utterly (*unimaginary*)
yet—

  Why, think this? How brake
The thought—

3

Start with consent. Then—
First, bent over my knees, let it—Then
  Not so much *kneeled* as
Knifed down (*prone*) lying flat,
  On my stomach, how I like it—Then
My body becomes *his* Observatory,
  Confessing Flesh—

4

why shames exist why sphinxes why want exist—

                                             O,

5

How I have wanted a Man to take me
  By the slight flare of my hips & spike me
To the Known Ground.

SOMETIMES TROPIC OF NEW ORLEANS, I

—Winter, roses all year!

The roses are in Love with the Warm rain today,
    And the white herons walk Easy down the Walk.
     What is a Life but its Weather? My Second Mind weighs
Already under this Given weather, bright as ravens squall
    Matter-of-fact fleeing on the hurt Night hour. Life thinks. Life, let it think
     it think. (Getting *Jussive*.) As a Heart thinketh may as well Be. Is there Problem
with the World where the roses Seem to Smack, Smile & Say
    Their hearty names? Yes. Apparently, Me. But I, walking, very Fallible,
    Delicious subject, pick one, among thorns, as to prove no fear.
I hurt. But I have problemed no World yet today for Being & ain't it
    Just lovely being Feminine, *Fine* and, God, I'm getting Meta.
    Call me *Rickey* Now *Riis*. Now *Obsession*. I'm that Horrible girl, Big honesty's spell.
    Like what I really hoped for was the menses Blood to drop, for Meaning
    To come severely across my life and be *Real,* initiation. But I could never be female.

SOMETIMES TROPIC OF NEW ORLEANS, II

7 a.m.-alarm fire, slut of fire, the Heron is a Woman in Red. I contract,
  I burn like the roses themselves
    & Compose my view, like the white herons are—Gay—?
  No, *Gray* But Now they teal. (*Trans?*) Now Oracular. Global Pandemic. The New World,
    Jealous
replica, Anxious enemy, is done: Let it *never* Get Done again!
  And I, Am urgently in—Today am I already in *The Next*
World. So they Teal. Now Blush-in-the-lip flies the heron. Now see I change (*You can*
  Really Change, y'all) their rosy color cyan, now pink, easy as I happen pink
Quick *quick*
in the poem coming as this Humming, wispy shower—I'm Another, passionately, like a
  Lover's brief asystole upon We meet.
Gay comes to Woman. Tho everyone can't
    be Trans. Everything I Hath
said in the poem Hath Happened in the poem: *Trans* commends *transition.* Now blond.
Transition implies *Passing,* implies *State Changes.* Versus blonde, Ice, now Speed of
  Orange. Really Roses! Rust, if shades maroon, if shades firepit fire's Red
    Roses (*writing* versus *singing vs. memory*) went the roses (*gender* versus *sex*) gone My mind.
    Each day is Storms coming by conflicted air's mandate: *All is Change & that*
  is Rapture; & is no Lie; taint, Nature, disaster; & ain't-black as them strange
birds.

BOY COMING OUT *GAY* GOING FAR TO *LADY* WAY TO *QUEER*

I confess the *Trans* is dangerous. It leans provocation
On the teeth of the mind: an idea, to kill all other ideas? like Category,
Order, Line? Suppose the Problem of the Century still
be the Color Line since the Problem is, increasingly, the line?
I walk my far lyric to self. Was I gay or trans, when? Will
I *Rickey* or *Key*? The Danger be if *Trans* willingly tear up and confuse all
Surfaces, & neat embankments and leveéd cities sufficiently
keeping one hood from another, what else? If you Look
at me liking what you See—are you Gay? Fag? Distinctions Bi? What am I
going toward once a Boy-going-gay (never Man) coming forth to Lady,
(few deny) for Queer's umbrella (gained) for Dreamed
Queen (all gained) to What else? Tho if I be Queer should Women who snarl
Love at me be lesbian, are Men who throw want at me straight? Carl,
I was gay my whole twenties & do I miss it but I miss the staying gay
after tongues kiss, that little Bottom Shame glossed in that name, Bottom.
Now Gay to Queer Miss to Dream to Trans*, all nice. Tho trans will suffice.

TIRESIAD: AUSPICES, I (ORIGINS)

    Logic gat-at proves—what, exactly? When
there were always myths? myths making sense of a Star?
    Equations
some Explain our Auspices eventually, their dark,
      Blacker, vaster,
if of Black-Hole privacies, *maybe*—not yet them Stars,
who Captivate, who pre-exists our calling them Stars; us,
    who pre-exist myth.

TIRESIAD: AUSPICES, II (DUTY)

"Old chips and sooty ashes on the altar," contaminate sky
—archaic fragment

SOMETIMES TROPIC OF NEW ORLEANS, III

Why is a Lie, Friend, anywhere in Poetry's charred category?
But Charm's their trade. I lie but when it *hurts* to lie (*See a bee*),
   I tell truths in their Species: what Shove its Hard, stinging knowledge, raw,
   down my throat, like sex do, or don't, or how doubt do. (*A bee considers,*
among roses, which rose.) Better I make this Baseborn walk meet my minds,
   transient Amateurs, if I can remember the line . . . an *Emily*
Dickinson poem? . . . the line: but can recall her Staggered gait instead,
What goes like the Sunday Organ: that Honest, afferent & mad. (*Among roses.*)
Can detect her Capital letters slam Accent, for Emphasis, & play
  Dynamic keys, since no *italics* can script
in cursive—These are blueprints for me, something like what I hope
  I really am. Or *seem*. Or *mean*.
But mark it against me, that I can but barely recall or write the *right* Emily
  Line, for my own digressions. (*A bee glides the felt of a rose.*)
Now this way I walk like a dream.

SOMETIMES TROPIC OF NEW ORLEANS, IV

Honey in my walk, & I lean, now down the Avenue, pseudo-pioneer to a seized
   City, liege to a bee—Say, Emily, what *do* you know of bees?
(*See the black Heron.*) I cannot recall. Didn't you write knowing
    the very Bees Spake and Holler in my ear for—what? Sensation's sake or
For to see?
    Orangest rose, I walk. (*Felt of a rose.*) I try (*Black Heron*)
   Not to cry this ecstatic world.
(*He eat the bee.*) I fear I have Minds mixed. Mixling, I do mixy things.
So this is why they banished the Poets from the Republic?
Poetry walks with me each step of my mad thinking. (He flies.) Poetry
   in Need of Rhapsodes again, Poetry must be slick
Comprehendible by the eyes *and* the air—that it dare
   Imitate a world, whether it be Making Confessions, whether it be Sex . . .
Sex is a Making Confession, where Love is; Art is its own Procreation—But I digress.
   With Stinging Consequence, Emily, all poems you left, trust,
are of much Consequence, weeping confession, justice, twilight. But, anyway,
   what should a Woman know of Sex . . .

TRYING TO MAKE MORE ENGLISH
(*OR, OUT AT THE CONGO SQUARE*)

—Twelve Antebellum Lyrics

1. LOVE POTION no. 9
Anyone I have designs on have 'em design on me.
    Let it. Let's make a good time outta a Tactile divine.

And Feel the *Crush* of that magnetism anticipate sweat.
    Let it sing poignant as the arriving rains, the Future,
Slams hard on earth to make a muddy Sound.
    Clouds, thunder. Yet a Church ruptures the field's scene—

2. SACRED PLEASURE (*CONGO SQUARE*)
—It be *that* beautiful, some Churches.
They loom your Minds with their needs of tithes, which is Indulgences
    interchanged for Shames, the receipt of no Honor . . .

But the trembling, powerful Body sometimes is a Church,
    when *trambled* with another:
        the bells of its shoutin' circles, ambling & concentric
(*versus* those twirling cries, darkening sky)
    (*versus* the dancing Spirituals & Quadrilles grandfathered into the Available)
the Bells *priss* with a Gospel joy.
The Python lives—

3.
—sealed in a Box, omphalic, pithiatic, sphinxlike lure:
That the Python lives.
So *priss, prass, hiss* is feminine language. Then *tremble, tramble, throb* is boy.

4.

The very Word attracts; its Spell go hard that we feel
Its almost Conspiratorial sense, in the mouth. Words want us *back*, and touch
Worlds . . . I think I heard a Priestess pray the World so opened the box—

5.

Black is a Native field! I see the field's opened box saying.
Beauty arises in trombones and trumpets regard,
With the world. O world O python that holds my eye like my man think me *fine*.
So the Decadent and Divine, like Sense and None of it, enjoy
Each other, enjoy many frictive Sunday episodes. And this is sex, before pleasure?
A mingled dance worked along the field of bodies? Say *Yes*.

6. ORGIA

Different from *one* body is
   (*I can sense their voice*)
The Body two bodies make,
   (*I can sense their voice*)
A tautology where a body's
   (*Their voice, present, mine*)
Fiction is argued fact
   (*Their voice, present, mine*)
Immediately inversed, as night is
   (*I can sense their voice*)
Today, tho some Native thought,
   (*I can sense their voice*)
Sees no distinction between Night
   (*I am native voice*)
And day, but is a Being
   (*I am native voice*)
A going-thru thru, Passed in-between.

7.

But I am between *eternities,* making myself Mesh.
  Speech is the Challenge toward more Speech, as Love is toward Love,
as Worlds . . . *Preen,* which is a girl's only last night's
  Cat's begging, hear it? She begged all night. Come from *Priss.*
Tramblen, another, further tense of *Throb,* ways from
  Tremble again:
Congo Square, then, with its hurt, trambled-down
  honor preens
with a kind of Carnival, surpassing joy; it wrangles the field.

Between the Decadent and the Divine, I meet,
  —shameless?—
Far from French, Spanish even,
    in the Strange experience of *Black* Englishes.

8.

  A church murders the crying field, so
Damn beautiful. Love—

9.

Love is a Python. A rising field.

10. THE FETISH FOR THE DARK

Let a girl sit in such world *be,*
  coy veil
  On her rambling beauty, gag set in her mouth—
So let the air splice & rise where
  the back-cheeks meet,

South, as she stares back in rewarding silence,
   beads all down her neck,
staring at the dark awaiting,
   Its only job be his needy entreaty, no robbery,
Tender & enter, me, Mister Dark.

11.
   Easy to see what walks out of Dark,
my Paw-Paw once said,
   But, What goes *in?* Designs,
They thrash against us, distorting History so.

Even now Middle of the Day, Smack Middle of old Congo Square,
   All sex still trespasses in a dark tableau.

12.
My mind be a pregnant thing. It labored this poem.

Mr. Dark, I got some designs on you, said I to the sky,
   Rain running down my hot face.

CREOLE LOVE SONG (*OR, DOWN UNDER THE BRIDGE*)

When you had gone the love came.
—EMILY DICKINSON

My boyfriend's anger come out in Dashed couplets.
  I'm a beast / I'm a beast, he raps, *I'm a tall*

  All
nigga. And I let him. *Yeahhh / Straight, racial nigga.*

  Yeahhh, he repeats, *Straight, Creepin' nigga.*
My boyfriend's anger trot out in Hellish triplets,
  And I would Kiss him

 Except not to stop his Cardiac Passion.
Won out in the strangest designations of his dark Soca
  skin O do I Love to Love it glisten, Love him,
Love being what he's owed, & me, his Passion got Up

in me as gaseous, delicious Heat, a star.
  Are we two Fetishes to the other? I hate
To think it. *Dark-meridian,* I have called him. *Light,*
  He calls me and something else. American *Negro,* once called us both.
And will we let it Sound again? But let me listen Not
  to absent his urgent song.

 Let my boyfriend's anger come out in sleepy quatrain,
  Tho is it my anger ever to explain?
No, but that I traffic in it still. Except I am already my own
  Proven boyfriend, my own family, own Shadow.

This is the story of a Mad girl wandering to belong.
Since nobody trusts a *Tranny* in this whole wide world,
     of course I have no boyfriend
Who is nothing but his rancor he has no Pride
     Left. No world

     Left. A man takes a woman, makes her his wife.
To take me me, he has no self-respect left,
     Says the world. So my boyfriend's anger come out
In this shaky quintet, & loud.
     Now I sit So next to me I forget myself,

So much in a tent revival of my keen, derivative sadness,
     A clear, returning Love. Except wouldn't him choose me broad
Daylight, if there were no fear? not someone near? *Don't fuck
     with me, baby,* Love said, *Baby, Ima come up.* Him said,

Don't fuck with me, baby. Let a nigga come up.
     And O! let it come true. *Uh, huh.* I would let me lean
On the Strength of him; baby, lean on the strength
     Of me. *Uh, huh.* And let us cling another,
Clung as the color Black is his song.

     Since everyone ignores a *Faggot* I became a *Lonely girl so* now
Will you Love me?

GIRL GOING BOY COMING BACK TO GIRL GOING WOMAN

T'ain't one & t'ain't the other, or something-like
Natasha said, and, I'm guessing, she didn't mean me, *X-
Going-XY-coming-back-for-another-X.* Maybe did. Supposing
we Must be always Enwombed in One mind's idea of sex,
that idea of Ourselves cautioned in our Mother's DNA, might
a Lady Person be permitted to change her mind? We *can* go back,
Go the other way, I say, all switch figure, & why not? So, Momma, let
my Body *thru.* Because Science? Medicine? Because I told me to?
Yes. But the help of Society are needs. Not construct, Gender
is a Social Contract, a laugh shared between different embodiments.
If the Mind alone make the Trans Decision, it still needs a *Body's* help.
Then I could be my own *Castas Painting,* discerning Mythy genders
over Mythy race. Then I would lend a painting's Lighted beauty
Out to the Society of the Body, where worlds blend and negotiate,
too, their component heirs. *You can get there from here*
tho *there's no going home,* Natasha said. Poem, let me *go* Home,
to that early circle, Cell, circuit, where there isn't contest & but *be*
the seed of a Girl. Whatever chromo vetoes it is No god, nor Oud.
   I am who I become & always been: fecund in the Belly, original Girlhood.

TIRESIAD: THE PUNISHMENT OF TIRESIAS, II

Now know the Gods require as much devotions
to their namesake as flame chews
   down the wick needs air to light the candle. Light the candle.
Ain't a 1:1, precisely, or Pound for Pound but there *is* a relation,
   Which strike a balance: "You will one day meet
God's sacral name you made together," Big Brass Snake says,
   "You will go out into the woods a Man, return
back a Woman."

TELLING THE STORY (OR, *WAY OF THE SERPENT*)

1.
My Sadnesses are Intelligent. They make
(by way of Chronic, hard Head traumas; Stress)
More, not less, Crooked in the Accidence of available Brain,
Apart from Heart. Tho the Soul survives this damage
Allowing me be smart, crazed, More broken but Possessable O
Of Myself—who Babbled English, Momma said.

I'm sad today, like most days. Am I really
Crazy or weirdly Depressive? Schizo or do I affect Small strange
Typos in Brain but grow reflexive? Diagnose me, please!
But aren't I sad my Momma and I don't speak the same
Artery; that my Hostile speech she wince at; my Chango'd
Soul bites her Ear. She repeats on me

As what cleanly quickfired Goliath, the Queen
Dido corrected by Pyre: neither tell their story. I mean she's meant
To call on me, her Black child, some umpteen times, the Cops,
Says the Record, to send me to Psych wards' dread. That's Not
My Child! Momma screams. Is it my fault the World brutalize
A change? the body's Elect?

Me, who kept getting hit?
Should've stayed dead, Momma never says, about my Career
Digression, my Life's Long Psychotic Sleep
I wandered on, sad Way of the Serpent, in a fugue, alone.
I babbled, she said. Days late. Didn't make no sense.
Didn't trust home.

It is sometimes the point of the Poem not to make sense.
It is not only the ask of the poem to suffer
An image of your pain and make that beautiful; sometimes,
Just to say what happened is enuf. Not to say they threw me
Back, strapped, cuffed, to a bare Twin bed, spread-eagle, & I'm not lying:
How three armed policemen & the white female

   Nurse that gladly jabbed my eye, left me
Shackled, alone, an X, hours like an ether, at University
Medical Center Behavioral Health Emergency,
Having replaced Charity after Katrina, having replaced Care,
At 2475 Canal Street, afraid as a child slave is
Afraid, Suite 2627, I remember, crying, no one's poet,
Only Singing loved me there, me peeing
All down my legs, their tawny lyrics, and they never
Told me Why or anything, or she explain. Not to make you care.

   My Sadnesses are Intelligent. They make
(by way of Chronic, hard Head traumas; Stress)
Less, not more, Crooked in the Accidence of available Brain,
Apart from Heart. Tho the Soul survives this damage
Allowing me be smart, crazed, More broken but Possessable O
Of Myself—who Babbled English, Momma said.

2. CODA (BLACKADORES)
   But I love her, my momma; she loves me. She loves
All her family wide—my brother in his teenage silence;
Ma-maw in her stubborn old age; and me in my adult obstinance,
my indomitability, makes a family.
The momma with her worried weather
Pleasures to cry her love, and I let her.
I wipe away, with one painted finger, most of her tears.

TRANS LONELINESS, TRANS EMBODIMENTS

—Martha P. Johnson

But *why* Doubt I'd *grow* Breasts a 'Natural' way?
Am I not 'Real' flesh? Am I not *likely* sway
Of the same species & given biology? Not Cis, you think me 'Alien'?
Scary? Do I so estrange? Must I be (*if seen*) seen like that Gorgon lady,
My two, New, *added,* latest 'Eyes' budding from the chest
Ache, O, it itched: the nips (*it eyes which makes a monster*) hiss & gaze *back,* best,
At a specious, Staring World (*its eyes which make slither*) feeds me down fists.
   So I took my Feminine *'chill,'* stalled burgeon,
Except for taking my *Antiandrogen,* patient, some several years, then 'broke'
   such 'Chill' to stern the Heart—that it?
Then asked for *Estrogen* (*eyes make sweet*); then I urged *Progesterone* into the Regimen,
All pills to advocate my Heart—indeed, I 'bloom'd.' Beware! I *am*
   a Beauty, with Spices added. I bleeds. See that I hope
Such medical, methodical 'Hormonal Surgery' put upon my Fungible flesh
   is yet—what? Enuf. And Assuming. Soy as I am & Black & coy.
Tho even Surgeries are our Due, Martha, *God's-child,* our Right to 'appeal'
& so Revise what Happy, lonely, 'Sovereign,' (*and eyes make holy*) Body
   we claim, I can't afford it. So I learned to express my Body piecemeal, no 'cancer.'
No coward, Didn't I rise in this a.m. to cry pearls? *Please,* friend; *Girl!* Answer.

STARING OUT THE PSYCH WARD'S WINDOW

The ravenous, controlling part
of the Voices coming was part
of the pleasure, arty, revelatory, & damaging; the Other part,
the vulgar, like freaky part,
was the Wanting it all over & Over & over again.

*

Headache. Twin, torn Black trash bags blown haggard got
Snagged in the bitter skinny trees now, a split second, be ravens.

*

Treasure,
what the leaky Minds can do.

CREOLE LOVE POEM

Are you bowed down in heart?

—JAMES WELDON JOHNSON

Downpour. Today just might flood. So my heart smiles down my body, modesty
   went, & going fast, & open-armed, sprawlish,
  & arches my back, heart twirling, dervish, and poised as if to catch the downpour,
      that Emblem of Love.
If it rained five minutes tho, *if* I ever find Love, *if* I feel so deserving, I'm a fool
   tonight: but it fell down
Hard-*hard*-Hard, flash storm, on the Roses, on every doubt, slicked the hair of
   the asphalt, glossed even the kid Magnolias across the way
it's been too damn Hot
   Lately for them to last their bloom, who try swoon anyway. I am Real as they, warring
with the weather, now bloodied, now watered by it, now preserved.
Love falls down, *hard,* eventually, the wind just barely assuming. Be not afraid.
   Go head let somebody love you, Girl! the Roses keep saying.

VERNACULAR HISTORY

mirage and myth and actual shore
—ROBERT HAYDEN, "MIDDLE PASSAGE"

Zipped up Gold in the dark Hold of some ship, what they did is Fly—
What they done is Cry, as far as Crave; didn't they Fantasize

              some Way,
Way back Home on the Continent? Such a *Choice* cargo, except
the Choice weren't theirs. No will. Except that bondage betrays, if absolutely,
the First Idea; nevermind, their Moan, their Soundings-out, I fear—

      But what if they *played*, with the Speech?
Out of dripping Need? if they *touched* each others' Sounds? & made them Ask
each other? Speak their name? So, Human ingenuity, not freight, shaped a Future
claim to this Language I treat
  as much, or even more than, pall gall England's.

Beyond the Physical sense of Life is its excess, is its Soul: see the Scorpion
Burst forth from the tongue's tip, timid animal, now raw, firing
sword, a weapon for provocation. Let not Myth be their name;
           Lend them their Ethics, their Arts;—

Let them their Ragtimes & Jazz suite already, at least some premature ghost
of her Blues, Big Band;—and let them *Read,* let Shade, with his hundred filed teeth,
  neat,
                aboriginal,
Packed Down-Bad in the Atlantic's roaring mouth, Rapping,
  Afraid to be afraid—

      But there is another view of the Trans-
Atlantic Slave Trade

that's just a view of one Boy barefooting
   some further Afrique Dahomey shore to see some ships' flags snap sharp
     & oddly in the wind, and certain Men
Who didn't have their color right.
Lipped up smart in the dark of that ship *Vague Wanderer*
   What to have but want a photograph's memory?
See it. Who can't see the boy's mother's hands, captive, beside him stretch hunger
   for that shit
Light—or hear in her falling sighs the Death of Ideas?

Let it be true: That at the bottom of the Ship is Still a Dignity *earned*.

       There is this counsel in my ear
That is my ear; that is my soul turned Maroon; that says a slave can't speak
   like this, think like this, cannot ascend,
      to be so-called "genuine."
But I say someone needs them to, I do, so I write it—
      Imagine

The imagination's power if made, this once, healthier with desire,
Not to raise categories, lines, enslave, or to kill—

      One could build a home then, finally.
One could resurrect a language light enough to fit our flying into . . .

TWO SECONDS THE SLAVE (*OR, CARNIVAL BABY*)

1. PREAMBLE

Suggestions *strange* upon my mind's screen I mean something sad.
You know what I mean, right, sweetie? Name's Dignity, Addicted
   Girl, Imagination; name's Key. No veil. No bells appeal the drunk air.
I am the grand, red Reconciler, the Songmaker,
   Diva, who gets things *Done*, Cruel Silk, Sweet Hurter.

2.

I was born Mardi Gras Day, Tuesday, *nouvelle créole*
   haunted in Charity hospital; that he was raised *almost* right.
Born Black, a Carnival Baby, I get a little ʒerk each orbit, which means gong-sad,
& Depressive. Their latest went quiet schizophrenic, very mad-
   woman-in-the-street jezebeling the Quarter deep, *deep*, thru its wide sternum,
of the City Municipal, a Square, a Star, a Snake.

*

Who's seen a Snake walk on two legs?
Walk down Bourbon's throat, turning right on Orleans Street,
   seeing each gaze remark it so
returned their gazes, held it high, whether straight, black, cis, white, or gay:
   I regarded each two pupils like two sorrows, I
inaugurated a special surgery on them, or Didn't, or just let them go
   thru *their* New Orleans, its tragic soul.

*

Walking thru my Crying pain made me *Crazy*.

 It made Language itself a god, with the Needs of describing my pain.

 I am the God herself of Rescued Language, or some'n like:

I argued onto each stranger their strangest *true*

and not dead name; it was gross pleasure. I told them where they failed, and also flew—

 their braggish, grinning slur, their hopeful

nobility's, superlative titles like *Darkest Creole of them All*

         *

Because I am tall, the re-inaugurator gets things off.

 Titles like awarded nicknames like you *the Duke of Truth*

or *Consequences,* Her *the Princess Submission,*

Him the *Governor of Black People's Culture thinking Ignoring Slavery's*

 Past, Filmically, ain't the Very Symptom of the dark

Slavery's Special mission

         *

not to See itself, critically, *Slavery's mean work, to Vagrancy, to Jimcrow, &c,* and Somebody

 Make a Movie already about Slaves & their Sex, like

(you *the Prince of Fascinations*) in the first few frames of Steve McQueen's

 12 Years a Slave (*you the Secretary of Yonic Suggestion*) that gasp! of

desperation! of strain! are they cargo of the ship? a dark-skinned woman's gasp

 as she forces

         *

 her way going up, Quick, over, & then downed

all of her Open self, over Him, Mr. Solomon Northup, so my Mind recalls,

 his brown eyes grown suddenly wide in apparent shock? happiness?

 or relief? or is it indignity, indignation,

at this treatment or circumstance that causes the Slaves'

 appetites, choices—

*

Or you to feel, voyeur, hot shame, offense, to lose
One's apparent way in the voyage, as to lose honor, Dignity, sobriety, it does some trouble
   To integrity. But does it mar
One's Goodness? One's sense of their selves? Consent?
   She mounts him, at the bottom of the ship, I think, in the film, like screw roving down,
and Northup

*

   who was *born* Free, who was halfway in his life Suddenly changed, must drop
his Consent? his Guard? his self-Regard?
   It is rather like when Black men (*you, the King of Lies*) today appraise
my figure? my face? raze my future? & they wave me over (*me, the Bitch that Cries*)

*

shudder and I shudder that they shudder (*apparently retracting their attractions*)
   I nearly feel *most* alien, less-than (*as if that be true*)
not even *Human* really, or Heathen, "Unintelligible Beauty,"
   lower than an Animal even: the Dark men shudder,
like to return their very attentions, as if to delete their gaze, can do,
   and *unperson* me, I feel *Two Seconds* the Slave—

*

   absurd as it seems, I flinch, or I just feel trans lonelinesses again. I do everything not to
   show it.
Now you *the Lady Anonymous,* you, the *Light of Visions*
   & now you *the Duchess of Black People's Longing,* you, always,
(*looking up*) the *God of Terrible Work,* and you, *Viscount,*
   You, *who Suffer Tall Sluts,* grace, you *Tess of Trans*
Rejection, you, *the wedded couple,* Lady & Lord of *Stampedes*
   of,
you & you, & . . .

CONSCRIPTION

   Human intelligence as it is being Precarious, how funny
we Want of all possible minds an Artificial mind. The Lower
   and Upper brains, like two Egypts spanning the Nile,
Cannot explain but Wait, in Patient breaths, to see how this poem will end,
   tho its enthusiasm remains chiefly mortal, generated by these my Red hands.

   They painted themselves that way, early Egyptians, So early
that when all seven Cleopatras spoke of their Archaic precedent they meant them,
   who Stones-moved-by-slaves show painted themselves Red, tho who you know
is even Red really? Red's rare? They constructed an idea

   of the Egyptian from Crescent colors, and different from the Dark
origin they were fleeing; they raised obelisks, they rendered in the Pharaoh,
   Red and few times Black, sometimes Tallow, who was *not*
Osiris, who began a king, but made Pharaoh that first Son of Man,
   Son of God—as we construct,

today, around us, a more ethical, electrical slave, as we render what ways
   the Artificial will think *for* us, not *as* or *with*, doomly *of,*
Answering the many doubts of a pregnant universe, or history, or whether & how make
   a Southern peach cobbler. Of us, would you agree,

there is something always glutty & deranged & Compulsory & wants
Not to die, and so Sad (since even Art decays), and keeps Making slaves?

HERMAPHRODITE! (OR, *SACRED PAEON*)

All Eyes on Earth be urgently Attracted to
that Hermaphroditic form I longed for having.
I have it. An Egyptian Hapi. Derision won't change the Body I swarm;
Nor Scorn, nor More Violence, or Lies
Can try me Small. I ease around, Quasi-Quadroon
   Of Sex's quick Ball, très Black, confronted with these added Eyes
Batted against the temple Grace of my Body, my breasts—
   O am I a looked-at Dignity! demanding yet Song!
That tight *thru-space* between Seer and what's Seen
Might be Sensation's rise, or Shame, or *is* Solicitation's chance,
   that calculus's arguing gender, sans
What petty, nubile Knowledge divides my thighs. *Remember me,*
the god Phanes, who created, cries; *Use me,*
   the god Hermaphrodite, who revises, replied:
I am Their audience. Honey, ain't nothing here subpar!
Light breaks over all Eyes like sound plays the Guitar.

FREAK IS A PRAISE WORD

—the Lady Chablis

Like *like* too freely writes the mind with such scrying regard to Life's complex differences,
   so that
like is likened to an enemy, right? I am not *like* a Lady, but a Lady (*claiming Title, Her Graces*)
   outright.

   *

Nonsense is the mind posed at times into Lyric gibber, distinct from Poetry, as the difference
Between Song and Treatise is Poetry is Voice. I'm the Freak that rewrites the
   Natural Voice . . .

THE MUTILATION OF THE FATHERS

As Saturn did his only father, who was Heaven, castrated Heaven,
    Seven angers drove Jove to reduce Saturn, too, by vigorous surgery. Cut
    to: Blood; Foam. His dick thrown to the sea sprouts the Fury and the Sex of Aphrodite.

      *

    Venus, Sea-walker, bring the downy light of Phosphor in the East, free Persuasion—

AT VOODOO LOUNGE

You have to really trust someone to let them all in your mouth.
Creole songs, who lets who out? It's not a short step from there
   to the False belief that only by the Suppression of
the Erotic, Lorde lectures, within our lives, Lorde begs, and of Consciousness,
   can Women's bodies be *truly* strong. Was she wrong?
But what's Strength's Speech to given Beauty? Character? What's
   Romance? Where do it lay if I *play* the weaker,
my Back broken in, for him, and I *like* it? I like my sadnesses
Swell, and gladly transpierced, the Subtlest inversion. I like the power these cheeks
   make impressionable on like a Scene for a Painting turned Rigid as he pulls
My hand to his now-less-lonely Manhood at Voodoo Lounge, fourth red seat
   from the back, at North Rampart between Saint Peter
and Orleans Streets, smart man. What Conquest's singing? So I like that suede
Way my suasion be killing 'em, lethal silhouette for these symptomatic men,
   Burn for burning covenant; them hungry, like fish-on-the-line, who Lean
a *likely* Swagger back. I see it by that pressure I'm building in their Eyes:
   It's what makes Kept men melt, run Clean up on me, Shouting my worth
that I do receive. Yes. *Yes.* Kiss me like I'm the Last Woman on Earth!

LOOKING AT SAINT LOUIS CATHEDRAL

—1788, *First* Great New Orleans Fire

O! the White sight of it splintered my sight some'n sweet, other Eye
    Gothic, for the Mind recalls The Slave Block raised behind her a century
of doubloons ago; my Mind can't forget traffick of the swart Afric'd, despite
    its sterling Beauty . . . I take my time tho, getting back to its Tarots & Lesser Eros,
coming from pink Old Algiers, *across* the River, now Lazing on a white
    College friend's wide porch, soon not, & with my Best face painted right
on &, fam, I shall want *without shame*. Swim! fly! I aim to down the freakish,
    mud divisions gat between Mystery & Obscene, Love & Loss, the Five
Pleasures, The Two Sisters, Use & Claim, Man & Woman. So I want to *Eat*
    the Cathedral Up as I Look at it; stave it past my mouth, hook it,
its Image, like to the gushy-pushy Heart (*Shame wants.*) that, like the Fetish,
    holds news—since what else is there? chainmail? some blood? *Fie!* ain't it
Wrong such *sweet* Aesthetics come sometimes Costly with ghostly appetites?
    Why do this, Beauty, what I want of Love? But History's glut, ain't I *likely*
-made, yeah? too Stunning for Love? that all men Sneak & say I Attract
    Too severely? & just Siren-Eyes? just Gettin' jussive. So, a freak, Blank, *nasty* desire now
      blackens my *look*,
Now I'm Gentler aim's & so I ask *Why is the Cathedral so*
blindingly-at-Noon white when fact
    is that Slave-dark capitalism had it raised? Who burnt it down? Who raised it up again,
      Spanish, right by soot?
& *but Why* must I adore it? Shame's back. When I sat on top of him, my panties a trace deep
    pink, ass fat,
thighs straddling his pelvis such we made a Cross, our Eyes gloss & make *Fairer,* still
    Godly, Dark, *échangées,*
that He came, a most Terrific Seizure, that He stuttered, like Rain on Lace,
(*Love me, a Voice cried*) the Sads came after, & only from *looking* at My face.

TIRESIAD: AUSPICES, III (ENCOUNTER)

So menaced, I made known a specialer, secreter name for God: *the One who Sees me—*

TIRESIAD: THE PUNISHMENT OF TIRESIAS, III

As soon as that dark Dye dyes its Black color manifestly on her Image,
So soon she is she conceived *Manto's* mother, Tiresias is, Omen of a Crone with child.

TIRESIAD: AUSPICES, IV (BODY)

Do I complete a Lover for the Gods now, the mortal Hermes, Tiresias, writing to the
   Oshun?
*If I speak the Words thru my Half-face covered in a Veil, the Libyan-lined Eyes irk you, the
   Words avail—*

VULNERABILITY (OR, *RIDING WITH DEATH*)

—(twentieth century, *acrylic, crayon, canvas*)

Then I could make each wound itself
An eye, a womb, a way of
   Seeing out upon
A world that did act
   Against me, yes, left some injury—

Him my harshener, my ride or

   Who I truly fuck with
I ride him from the zero's place, all bottom,
   that know, can
Know, this way to pretender's seeing,
   A grammar. I mean,

I fuck with his sin, first word

   For blood, like thru that canon law
Would find and did right friendship, Wealth,
   Rest, pleasing repetition.
Did I know him as a music then?
   No. Call it the Law of Caught Mirrors,

Moment when, no awkwardness,

   One face faces the other and together
Seem to say *I'll make*
   Some infinite, repeating more of you—that's

True, right, that's half a reason why
    I even care look at him, my eyes, these wounds

Of power. Attraction is

What sex claims to be. Is that it?
    But I wonder why my eyes do work
Like this, fit, attracted,
    To the shapes of things first—shape of his body,
Or how he's some black Atlas

Shouldering that shape and me

    Calling the burden Beauty. *He fine*
As hell, one tongue calls another,
    Speech or intimacy,
It doesn't matter. But, trust, I'm fine as well,
    Again this breed

Of grammar, to lie and let

    His nerve, his honesty, slip servile
And hard into what mirror
    My interior holds. What we have is
The body. Is that it?
    Like my body were some ancient well

—*inverse* tower—as in *Orvieto*—
    Where I summered at, no more for Water than to loiter
    Some prayer or refuge in. Never
    Mind. I think you know the drill: *Come in.*
You only need take each stair, stone by stone, to travel half
    The double helix, toward that bottom's

Friendship, damp, maddening, and deep

   As dark does go to make all shapes irrelevant.
Is it the dark, finally, the one shape
   We can know? Is it blackness? Should I
Turn up? Dare I disturb the lights?
   Who I fuck with is not so much or only

A matter that we fuck, or could—

   But that he leads me
To the root of the word
   Vulnerable, which is myself, and bid me
Kiss it. It's possible the dark
   Does hold at once, and easily,

All simultaneity: to live; to almost die;

   Shadow and be
Dead; faith; apology; time. Let him press himself further
   On my vision. Let him
Deeper scar me so with my consent.
   Then I will know
Freedom in the shape of his body.

   How his arm swung casually at his slick,
Most naked side becomes
   My eyes' theater. Him that eases me, I truly
Fuck with. Is that it? I see now
   How the veins of his forearms come up

To the very surface of my seeing

Requires kind desire ode from me.
Death is revision. That I would bray like a bucked consciousness
    And animal gold. I know
This time, afterward, he lets go his thirsty hold of me,
    Moment when
He turns away his face,

    His front entire, stretches, rises, so that his back,
The very crown of shoulders, stands
    Up, apparent,
Basquiats above me, it is strength,
    Finally, not failure, not abandon, I'll see.

How the deep melanin of his skin

    Repeats me. We are not endangered.
It is not always true nobody knows
    My name. Once, I admit it as the cruelest joke
That I be called to him, or any man,
    When it's been

Black men's masks so long

    Hurt me. But look
How even the hair clevers down his jaw, speech
    Or intimacy, sharpens
Against my cooing touch I say is infinite. Such I see
    It's some hurts could be welcomed, yes,

The idea one needs,

    Or is it a question—
What would it beg you do, really, the right Freedom?

TIRESIAD: THE PUNISHMENT OF TIRESIAS, IV

Called to Heaven, the Augur, Tiresias, must profess
Which, between the two Sexes, enjoys Sex the better (*this is true myth*).
   So for his answer is damned & blinded once by Juno, rapt
& gifted a greater foresight by Jove. What the woman took, the man gives.

TIRESIAD: AUSPICES, V (MANTO)

So, the stork bird flies in the middle of the air—
So, I, Tiresias, some nine hours later, have Labored to bear and birth
   the shrieking caul: the Covered babe, the Seer child, Manto—

SOMETIMES TROPIC OF NEW ORLEANS, V

Why is a Planet so Damned to heat that the Herons get
ever encouraged just to withstand it? What is so secular to look at me
    and think me Brave heron just to *be* seen? But
aren't the Roses tachycardic & Divine still? Don't they
just make you smile. But not me? They bloomin'-bloomin', and I smile
    Pedigree to no one, peer to the Sun. What love
we have, what deep Color. What a joy it be to be alive, corpuscular, and final
    Heaven, wild even just to suppose it, to seize at life like they very Earth siege the day.
My idea of Color is like sensation & Whitman Big, I spill over.
    My very Feelings have gained a further floor.

But, the very Roses are not Palatable zones upon which
    I perform, most indecently, a scrutable dialectics. She is not Text.
The Rose exist that they exist, and groomed by the thorn
    Themselves they need no defense like "What they really call you?"
And "What you really is." You is what you be. All the Roses starts as seed,
    Seed to Stratify to Sprout, beating-hard, that when the wind
Strikes, it strikes the petals of the Rose like the Soul plumbs its messy Heart
    & no one ever asks why. Hardly can; should. *Why do you exist*
isn't English.

The Gods all need their names said back, devotionally;
Like the two hisses, hissing, do miss another.
Now she, too, needs herself returned a ways, to a time before gender.

TIRESIAD: AUSPICES, VI (ORIGINS)

I wasn't myself before I was myself.
You thought you knew who you thought you knew.
   No serpents.

USE OF THE EROTIC

I want to be an honest man and a good writer.
—JAMES BALDWIN

I like the red that hides itself, coy,
In a library quickie, thru pages, that mahogany
Hold, and I love the skin mahogany.
I like the specifically wet pink of my lips
Before a kiss, or after biting them,
Anytime I'm thinking or nearness ends.
I like the even way such *ignorals* quit,
Like brown eyes turn to honey
In excess sun. I like the way the dark
Entwists itself to ouroboros and indigo,
The crusher snake, and someone's possible
Being there, a being-also, in the room, beside you,
Not for scare, but care of you, and I like
A look of agony. Except some way East Asia's
Hair sheens to comet blue and cobalt averno:
I like that, too. I like the hue of my hips.
A haint is just most any saint with a hint of
Ghost, like how in the selfie, to the right,
I only see the charred ghost particulars
Of his face smiling to see me. I like to see me.
I like to be too thinky, kinky, and thinking about
The very Colored smell of just-cut grass,
And the better tale of it after it rains. I like
To like the things and people and blush
And have designs for and go *Oh Lord*
And appetites and be resigned to the crush
Of this power, and to trust it feels good, is
Information, a fat color, quarantine, the weather
Of a new hungry sun. I like to say "Aubergine"

Over "Eggplant," and "Negro" over "Négro."
I like a dick that stands right up at attention
And points its mention, its being-hard, very
To the one it sees a door, I mean I really like it,
Eight inches, Mister Dark, and the hum of that seeing,
Drum of adore, which is the color of his head,
both heads, thinking—an easy brown, a snare,
A truffle, and weird luck. I really like to fuck.
I like the color swear words make fractals
In my mind, and it's a shame cotton fields are so
Pretty, a very haute green. I like the color wags
In a Puerto Rican flag stood up in every window
That, of course, ain't Puerto Rico. And the literal
Black, when it's clothes on my skin, which isn't
The literal black, Vantablack, but something
Like mahogany again lost of its darkness, which I love,
And a creepy yellow melody replaces my face:
I like that. I like to spell Hawai'i like it's spelled.
And I like a yellow halo more than any yellow dress,
Tho it make men fall clean of their bikes;
I like a good fight, and any yellow *Yes* sworn
from the Better Goddess returned from Hell. I would like
To be so honest and a good writer, without this being-man,
And indigo's soul, and the quieter arts, & men, like windmills,
Blurring. So "petrichor" is a word that feel "grey"
To me, not "gray": I like that I hear that like I like
My syntax. So Oshun is a name that feels bronze
To me, which is the better call of my skin, tho I know
Here's ignoring gold. I like the way sounds do come,
Cum themselves, like crying do, that second ejaculate;
that they become their colors, immaculate, colors
Cum their words. And I like the color flying
away of almost any bird. I love this world. I love this world.

THE VAGUE YEAR

(OR, *AT THE END OF THE WORLD MY LONG PSYCHOSIS BEGAN*)

The pistol was at her temple. She dead. It was when I had nobody. This is a story refuses explaining just yet. Anger, lately. Roves and stores of anger. ("She's still a man!") That night *he* created out of me a rival, Black, *Male*. I vagued my transitioning life. You'll come to understand. Night of my assault, K.B., who had gotten that name in prison because he was told he wasn't like the *average* White bread, was handsome, but often grim, salt-and-pepper; a White man, whose family weren't from New Orleans like mine, but, let's say, from the Carolinas or he was Virginian. Cornbread was Virginian as he walked in; his appetites were. Gabby knew.

Just two girlfriends fanning a friendship or trying to, like a green fire, platonic, between them, interrupted by a Man's carnal suspicion. (*Steal away.*) But Gabby didn't know our secret. We were at the Old Base in the Bywater, an abandoned former Naval Base by railroad tracks that spanned over three blighted warehouses, with sea vessel abutting, what looks out to the Lower Ninth across the Industrial Canal. It stands right at the corner lip of real sand & stuff, a pop-up beach, cutoff by some Wharfs that go as far as Jackson Square. The Square you know, but not the Base, covered in graffiti, and looming. And for a certain cross-section of the population, ravers & dog walkers who enjoyed the natural levee that followed the Canal into the River, and punks, poets and artists; but for the *locals*, if no one Native to the city, the entire area, which, besides the warehouses, included tennis fields, a parking lot, a defunct petrol station, all of this was called, almost appropriately, *the End of the World*. At such End, the Base housed, illicitly, in camped-out rooms some filled here with debris & there with extravagance, the squatting derelict, punks & trainhoppers, runaways of the law, disgraced veterans, too many daddies, just enough whores, all beggars of a Creole society, and no one Creole.

Unless I was one. My family counts in the Crescent city an entire century and more, and I was born here. Not them. They jumped traincars coming from places like New York, Florida, Chicago and as far west as Oregon. Drawn to it by a certain kind of craving, I came too some days, some nights, because some days, some nights, I was someone exiled by their trauma. And might the dark be trans girl? We came, each lured by the Mississippi River, with its many Soothsayers, and to some private mystique of the city. A child, I never knew of the dark allure, or the veil exactly for the veil was always thin, wind that pulls talk of the city to its eventual initiates. It was like the menace of those Naval Bandos, which never dully registered, that came like hearsay: that ghosts stalked its halls, some spiritual, but mostly addicts; that the squatters there scraped its very walls for copper & nickel & tin to sell at the Yard, for to feed their addiction; and that, in the lower basements, was its danger, or where they stored the bodies after, so the rumor went. Devotees of a dark otherworld & its gods, in other words, a lawless hive. That night, his three punches didn't humble me. Can I explain it? Can I explain desire?

You should see a Spooky, Green film dress the story, suggesting addiction, small fear, vulnerability. He hit me. He projected on me jealous intentions. Something about his Generation or one before, made challenge with direct speech. And my body was speaking, Black, and its other shame: that it was Trans. His girlfriend, Gabby, sat in her corner of the room, suddenly not certain of our friendship, suddenly she knew our secret. We were iced out. So that's when I didn't do it: Scream, because why Scream yet? I

didn't cry my anger, not yet indignation, not yet even flurry or fuse. I was merely confused how Someone I would have just a moment ago called Friend was not an enemy against me.

His hits weren't working and he knew it.

"Nigger!" But I don't know the word registered.

If we were two men, we would've been in fisticuffs. But it was just me, against the Virginian, two sides of the track. I wanted to go Home. I was in a Bad, Bad way. A pistol? Or gun-shaped torch, to bring me burning to a star? Already in the stairwell, *something* brushed my head that it made me stoic. I had just visited, bringing the couple maybe things they needed, Christ-haunted, some soap, canned food, and batteries. Why was I so haunted, except that I was lost? But I am no one's Messiah, when I walk it is not on water but on the simple asphalt ground; Marys do not beseech; Friends don't Hatch down the roof and lower a Fourth man down, in his bed, sickly, to the Lord's healing. Yet I was myself some kind of miracle, something requiring belief.

I'm not asking you to be identical or have the same life as me, same pain, but to recognize pain in your own family, name it, and sympathize. I walked with my own permission to be there, haunted vaguely, wandering the City like an echo, in a strange fugue state. But I wasn't writing my own gospel, vaguely or not. It came after the lockdown year, the Pandemic. The Vague Years originally meant a few conflicting things to the Egyptians or the Romans, whoever, instituted its calendar, slag over those months out of sync with the Equinoxes or was it the Poles? when a single Summer extends hazy & tense over all & thruout the years of the story like a sun staying up all day, all night. This is a story make a Nigger weep, or not, weep right into a further, future America. All the vague year, I went wandering, a wandering lady going back and forth from Home, where the Family missed me, where the Family doubted & mistrusted me, back to the Ole. But when The Virginian called me ("Man") I didn't wince ("Nigger") because I know what I am, or was learning, and, still stoic, never agreed with his insult.

I may have laughed even, the indignation rising. "Go on! Let it all out," maybe I hollered, "Show us who you are!"

Get-go at the Base was all unbelongedness, for we were all lost. We all felt it with the world for a thousand reasons. I felt it for being seen with little sympathy, large desire. In the Long Psychosis of my head, Christ comes with the Oshun, with the Father, who play a trick over my head, their Voices now brusque, now slowly, now inviting counselors. It was like Isis, who speaks from her own Voice. Just who was I to them, or anyone? But, to the Virginian, jealous, I was something executable for desire and I threatened. I tried make my way. Sympathy is only afforded to those who didn't have a choice of the lot, in which case you don't *sympathize* as much as *pity* them, I would find out, a position of some privilege if it isn't power. I tried make my way. In the stairwell I was with the feminine Wisdom, that holy ghost comes thru like a secret, but without my booted heels, I had been wearing, even without my glasses so that I could not rightly see. My only defenses were speech. ("Stop, please!") Or the secret. ("Now I have to *kill* you!") And danger was right at my nape. I couldn't think of the time of the secret, or contemplate guilt; I turned to face him. You see about your kind your kind *cracks* at the slightest, or severest, of changes: that "*tranny*" way some of us would be purged of the weird first condition of a body, challenging fate thru a challenge of Gender, if not upon our Sex. That society wounds, those of us lost or found within our bodies, that we wound ourselves: this much remains but we might diverge toward a future where we purge, in toto, the wound itself, even its idea. I had been gay first, that was the idea, and wounded flesh, before becoming a woman; becoming a woman, I was some strange edition, trying to heal, & out of their makeshift apartment of a kind moved with deathly calm.

I remember, for the calm, I felt like
something dispossessed. I saw his Eyes
razor me with belligerent attention,
tweaking addiction riding the both of us
hard. Only his was Adam, well after Eve,
and mine some androgynous Adam you
read of just before her, still privileged to
name the world which included them.
In my body, it was like I occupied some
coming body, yet still myself. I was Her
one angle, at this precise second, a split
second more, and turned just so, now
He flashed across my face: I recognized
this, yet I was still myself. The self is
something bound up in all its history, both
private & secular experiences of a life, so
cannot be lost in the human.

Transitioning made me vulnerable
to twisted or anyone's interpretations.
Reinterpretation of myself and its
attendant questions happened all at
once & also gradually & were hardly
quitable; some homelessness did, too.
And it was like a city of homelessness at
the Ole, everyone dread with a leprosy
that keeps you from & invisible to the
city proper. Now, where I had made petty
community, where I had come down to
listen, even here I didn't belong. Now, as
too many time, prior I absorbed violence
born out on the face, the fact even, I had
changed.

Police come after the story, attempts
to reconcile with the Family, still after.
It was difficult work gaining sympathy.

For always I felt harassed by the notion
I was not myself someone to be trusted,
open deception. This is a story refuse
explaining *why* I changed, just that I did,
not how, but exactly when. I could have
started us earlier, before my Vague Year,
when time moved linearly and like empty
prose. It was back when I was somebody,
celebrated, honored. Yet something had
made the Cisness crack from the Body, to
one thousand shards, that it scatter open
like as many doors, each door an Orisha,
a guarded possibility. But when I gave up
the ghost, I think, I most was changed.

Or is it essences, the idea of essence,
distinct from the career of one's soul; or
is adopted character, or simple title, that
had changed? when I realized was my
truest authority is my one body surely it
is also mine to steer, nourish & to repair
& to refix as it needed. I was all of my
own responsibility, put her to learn from
trauma. But society prefer you regret the
body, repressed by its trauma; preferred
you suffer quietly within it, over taking
divers or even radical aims. But society
was all out there, I had figured, where
New Orleans sweeps into the Marigny,
the French Quarter & more. It judged
you for how well you kept to its designs.
("You're still a man!") But now it meant
the Virginian, toting a weapon, writing
violence, for his own berserk reason,
against me.

So this is how an anger creeps into the

language, hanging over everyone, a panic that spikes the blood.

Not yet the repose of my soul, a crushed indigo, with some gun pointed to my head. I'm a changed woman. I wanted to have said. Pistol at my head. Three clicks were fired; three, misfired; three days sojourned in a Catholic hell. I wanted to have said, "Are you done?" in my slow voice. At least I thought I said. I saw pane of a cracked black window, explain the crack. See along the edge of it still cracking, to a wider frame, which was the window's report of the Far river, Dark river, and Free. Black as the river is cracked pane, that at one exact angle is a Black mirror: a nearer & nearer, jagged flash of my face. But was it my face? Or someone culpable? Now a ghost? Now a dream? (*Steal Away.*)

Now Yemoja, Queen Orisha, waits in the dream, while ships with names like the *Going Imagination,* and *The Rose,* carrying a delicate nation, sails the stormy Black Atlantic in divine time—*Umoja* is a Swahili term means *unity,* but it arrives in Yoruba more closely as Yemoja, big with the belly, dark, the mother of Oshun. Mother *snapped,* like Sethe did, half crazed & shrillish crying, snapped in half—for to follow her stolen children in the wakes of those ships to the Americas. Since then, all our Ori on our Heads been left for Dead, so that I am left only a Soul, two or three Minds. She,

who presides over the upper surface of the Oceans distinct from Olokun, guardian of the Deep, snaps as to duplicate herself with all her selves, ones back in Africa, ones across America. For protecting Black ingenuity, not just Pain, she arrives as the Virgin. At the Eastern shore; in the Gulf, she gives birth to a tricky future. See thee Oshun, her daughter, a river, with weepy eyes throw. This is an Initiation. Be in syncretism with a *Catholic* Holy Ghost! Industry! *Shake* ya Ass! Laveaux & Louie don't be a Zombie! Have Purpose! Be Devoted to the Rivers its many Tributaries and *Have* Mass! Child, Praise their Names! Recall!

I was as a Bronze American Person so recalled, less than Black, and you can join me—well, not here, not literally, at New Orleans's old abandoned Naval Base I have said that hugged the Mississippi River, who is also a God (*the Father*); alone, I was with my God (*Thee Oshun*) when I idled into a tricky crisis God (*The Christ*) with myself witnessed that violence punctuated intermittently to manufacture Divine (*The Holy Ghost*) promotion (*Thee Oshun*) of the Soul. Black mirror (*The Christ, The Father, The Oshun*), now the shape of what punched it is the window gaping. I could see out into its History. All this, more or less, in a second. Me still walking priestly-still, down, why wasn't I running? But a felled Angel feeling finally shook forth—*as* my

wings, psychically, and I was saying it was
when I had *No* Body! I was shocked calm,
clean, calm as these concrete stairs the
military must've first poured a few years
before 1919, then what, then Prominent
again the Second War, 1940s, then gassed?
by the enemy? Gas must've let those
poor men dropped down Dead at their
desks, a few chance objects still marked
the Complex exactly as it would've,
may've, been, pens turned just which
way, scribblings of reconnaissance,
I suppose, still drafted over their
chalkboards, and a calendar where the
year 1966 is circled, when the Base was
transferred, renamed, renamed again,
deserted for the Other Side of the River,
Federal City, so that what remained
was sold to the City, left bare, privy to
prying need, or punkish leisure, graffiti
again painted across every wall, each
staircase like this one which I descended,
priestly-calm, stilly, still with—well, it
wasn't my Body. Outside, New Orleans

was still itself, in a tense sense, but I
wasn't my eyes turned toward the River.
I was something else, an about-face,
transfigured, maybe, a Swan, something
funeral sweeping the levee; something
else thanked God and turned its gaze
out for what is finally *not* the End of the
World for there are peoples, red or dark,
farther than, who live that way, & further
than the limits of tragedy; black families
who survive. Something else regarded the
sentence I had walked out of as I was out
of my shook self, the changing body, and
out of experiences, and dead. In life, there
isn't an Ending as much as a Crossing,
as much as a Going-thru a Purgatory,
becoming something less trifling, & Sad,
& Craven, not at all as you had been,
broken by the wheel, which is shame, tho
it became your Responsibility to mend, as
much as an X, what Death is, as much as
a passing Quietly into a secreter society.
(*Steal away, home.*) They never found my
body.

GOOD NIGHT

To be Edified,
> to be *Changed*—
>> Improved—

  *

To love after injury; as, after fault.

  *

   Now that I am Broken, that the Peace
Can (*Easy now*) slide in—

  *

But will you let the Potter break you?

  *

I know God is not *just* Man
That he should cry, should 'beg' *Peace,
Be still*—'beg' *tenderness*—to the winds
Their ever-unfolding argument
With the waves.
> Waves—
>> They—

  *

Just do. Have to. *Good night.*

  *

To love injury, even.
Injury, who delivers.

*

"No weapon formed
Against me can prosper," it's written.
Meaning: Here is my sword;
I have it, if useless now—

*

But I carry it.

ALL GOOD THINGS WILL BE ADDED UNTO YOU
(OR, *THE EPIPHANY*)

a voice begins

The first time I got hit I was torn to utter error.
The second I got hit I was so torn.
The third time I got hit I was torn to utter error.
The fourth time I got hit, uttering, urgent
Stop this! But no help, no letting.

Fifth time I got hit got me tore up, teary.
Sixth time I got hit fed me terror that the seventh
Made me weary, by the eighth, made me worn.
Now the ninth hit was so clean I seemed

Deserving as the tenth time I was hit,
Missed my eye, looked up, woe eleventh,
Didn't, stealing my wealth owed.
I will always see them see them hit me
'Til a Coroner's review. I will not coy; buckle, shut up
My gaze, or cite shame. Do not subdue. I am the first

Of my name. I prove some magic remove flesh makes
Into all-else, which is forgiveness, and make
Rigor my dance, wind back my woe, respool my wealth,
And just that sadly now—I know. And gall mood, moth & fly,
& brass incense the very grammar I speak,

The grammar hammer at me, *right now, like this,*
—Get it?—I try a *critical* resplendency, like gods do.
Like gods teach ash out of fire, now dye, now lye,
Clean in eleven cowrie shells sleep *aṣé,* and ain't
You some type of god some way *'cuz* you get it,

Got just enuf of my meaning, spindrift, to grab it.
You hurt with me, *me,* right now, uttering this
Make you hurt with me *some bad,* who studies
In pain, who can take it, who can learn the given
Instrument only hers to grab—take it up in air,

Wince, finding you will lose, done lost, must lose
Everything to fly in air, since flying hurts;
You hurt with me and, sufferer, don't need too long
To hurt, no one don't, like I don't need rehearse
My trauma specifically as the second violation,

For you to feel the hammer the twelfth hit hit
& I was told I provoked. O please reject or otherwise
Love me. The thirteenth hit went *Manic Ways,* and it was.
I learned. And became nice, creep & sensuous all air:
I am Caesar; I pass the Lady Chablis; La Sirene; Aquinas.

The Seth Head Animal; and I am the Public Universal
Friend; I am the First Musa, umpteenth richest
King of himself, with his whole whalebone for a back,
Brass gat up his cock; except I am Anonymous,
Who was a Woman, I am Saint Rita's Solitude, Nan Queen

Of Saint Malo's Maroons, Someone Surely Resurrected.
   My name is Boudicca. Do not subdue.

PASSION ISN'T TRAUMA ISN'T FURY ISN'T REPEATED PAIN

Blood stood up on her face shocked once,
Not again; never mind red be boring. Dreams, talons,

*

Not just some sutures, but dreams suffer my split head now used to
suffering red. Pain is hot, the sun, viral, so foul pain

*

Now is any random star, is all dwarf stars between us. Tho my face betrayed
none of their dark goings-on been faced, that heart

*

(*Beat face, by Stranger company, again & again*)
is scarred; survived. Baby, it throws me

*

left, & something hard. Am so *throwed*—
How once you come that far to know the growl beaky pain, you you know.

—*for not only Brianna Ghey, in memoriam*

CARGO FOR A SACRED POEM (OR, *SAINT MONICA'S PATIENCE*)

> Lord, make me pure but not yet!
> —SAINT AUGUSTINE OF HIPPO

1.

—Still *transubstantiate* is not a word I'd know describes
   Change, since it ain't Vernacular,
Since it means Eucharist only, that Ghost, thin & holy,
  Leavener & Host pulled slick on the wire
Wick longing intones our mortal tongues. Hunger sleeps
   unamong us each Sunday Morning then,
Still fasting, empty to receive initiation. I was only ten.

   Then I was only seventeen. I was Antique,
If I was Modern. I belong to that longing
  Mary knew, such honor & no pity yet; to those wide
Cups of sadnesses at her hips, fleeing Herod, and the altar
  Dresses, millennia later, my only pick to pretend
At being the Virgin. I swore that sharp, white skirt
  Bites at the Eyes; that in bright, excessive sun it gleamed.

   Then I was twenty-three. I belong to the ones
Who *do* longing now, yeah, yeah; lean
  Just like the Body of your crucified Lord, immortal,
Catholic, humble above me, and how my twink eyes
  Were early-on craved, cured, and scandalized
By his sexy Hanging there, Baptist Blood
  Where the side-cut wrote itself and Rome pierced in.

Salt spit Sprayed the Wet lips, too Wisp for me,
  At twenty-five; his body much too literally
Viscerally white for me, in memory, in *recent* history,
  At twenty-eight, I wanted him Blacker, coarser

Hair where the Image stained straight, but it's something
   about the cast-downward Lectern of
His hammered stare and His head, dead, veered down.

   I was thirty. I belong much more to the sound
Now Veronica makes when, stations before
   He dies, she takes a selfie of her vilified Lord with
The clean, cream cloth again but pressed to his red face,
   A maroon sound of fiction, and low, serious,
As the very name Veronica is low, and feminine,

   Or Magdalena, or Babylonia, or Lazarus's anger
That met me when I'm thirty-three. A wild wind,
   Like the lonelier pitches a harmonica aches,
The long way it steals air from us all
   But into itself and, shaking, cries. *I'm a Lie, I'm a Lie,*
Lazarus wails, *to be brought back here, Mad,*
   from Perfect peace! A wild wind worked my mind.

Hell, even Hell is a Peace not mine. I was less & less
   Contemporary; my progress confessed
Sorer than a line and I ideated. I believed everything,
   Now Piéta; now Anne & Joachim;
Miriam; now Hagar is still an Egyptian slave & I make
   No sense to the Family, tho my Patience
Begins a future. Now Kore; now Girl Assumed

   By the Father's Sinister Hand, lately Sapphire,
At thirty-five, now Virgin again, who is Attended by Roses
   Riding St. Expedite's seas; Blue Lady *Mami*
Wata: Do I Belong to all Hers, too? I think I believe I do: to Her
   Lourdeses & Sophiae & blesséd Louisiane & Ports
of the Ocean where Sirens sleep, from which one done snap,
   Has snapped, & will, & right at the fin,

For following her Hollering motherly instinct: she do it,
    Yemayà, fleeing Kings, to follow her sad, stolen
Children, slaves dragged across centuries, ridiculous cargo
    for a Sacred Poem, yeah, yeah, nevermind
It made & remade America. I belong to these, Her voices,
    Singing mourning, lonesomely,
In her Black child's ear found like at the bottom of Lake Lanier;

    Or to the crooktime come again, some stations yet
Before, *before* Yemayà is left out of the story, like Mary left
    Out of the story. Couldn't be there when Peter
Tries his thrice denial or the trial with Pilate or the Iscariot kiss.
    But when Missus Immaculata arrives
As the merely Convenience of her weeping only, and becomes,
    Like a stream, brilliant, stoic, and so lonely

 In herself to be rocking her dead son in her limb arms,
    How Black is that, how very Black Historical
Is that: *that's* when I conflated Gods, thirty some'n else,
    Why I syncretized a New Religion upon my Body whole
To make of myself an Easter. But it is sometimes warned a Soul
    Must let Fall, always, itself; must come to its most
Earthen'd state, which is Sex, which is Black,

 In order that you be Preferred, & further Heaven.
The Lord gives way His body, the Goddess gives back.

2. PRAYER

First nail, the nail; then *Noli me tangere;* then, *Touch me.*
We are Keys. Do not wrong me. The careful moan. We
Must know ourselves. We must let us know ourselves.
We must know we to each other Can agree & on ourselves:
That we are always Gaining on what we Know. Let it.

YOU WOULD BE CHRIST

Love bade the men to boat and sent them over,
And love sent my Lord up the mountain to pray. And love lent
The old moon down to him, extolling loneliness,
While the boat made way long way into storms, the wind dividing the waves.

And love returned my Lord back to us, walking the division.
My Lord on two feet walked the sea. Tho love fell
once the men could recognize him, so fear said: "Our Lord is dead."
   "No," my Lord disagreed, "I am not the Ghost." He said this, encouraging our love.

I was Rock.
I was pulled Rock then sent in fierce recommendation. My soul stood.
Then walked the waters too, separate from the men.

Still wind was all indeterminacy, bitter gossip, denim, sienna,
and like the waves my love wavered, like a flame. I was sore afraid
but made me say it, "I need you," when my Lord's hand replaced my doubt
   for that final help, that perfect help, the first—

Love, then, became the very boat we entered again;
was all the men's true witness, X, was wind dividing the waves
such that I felt no wind, no distinction from the waves. Storm reformed.
I had been this side of, you see, now I was *thru*.
And Love beyond. And Lorde.

RIDICULOUS ACHE, RIDICULOUS PATRIARCHY

Nigh the end of my twinkdom I dommed
   for no one, per usual. Was the advent of
that Open questioning, God-awful
   Flashback

   To a Tall Opus, Rich, far-from a Lady,
But when I played one—not in 'Gay
   Poems,' if still to Much applause. Motels
saw my Ache to make Use of

Some slick, Ordained, *Straight*, Male
   licentiousness, that stains Desire rust-
Orange, antsy, faggy Red, burning-crisp former
   red, rouge, to Violation, seething
hottest blue,

And honest navy passages,
   Desires desperate, in my Queer way,
to upend Power, Conformity—
   All men are melancholy after Sex

   But it was Really power upended, real blood
Plumming my lips: Power, as (*once ago*) a Gay Bottom,
   To bend at conformity, so-called Morality . . .
I'm sick of Christian succor, Christian help.
   It gets us nowhere, lets no one
Reconcile their Desires. But to see the men Sweat

yet a Womanish suggestion
Subject, drawn, unto my Body was enuf. But Men wanted more.
   It made me feel to almost Belong—
To what? I don't know. It made me feel.

That their strong arms rushed at my waist
   was the taste of a New Covenant,
relevant to just Him & Me, just Him & me,
   Power rotary like an engine's Pistons.

We are not Contradictions, one & the other,
   of each other. But are on a Spectrum between
Man & Woman, Masc & Femme, which make false Polarities,
   And get Various treatments of a Wicked fire

   That Attraction starts as. God won't be cured.
Loneliness? It can. That I pulled them
   Legitimately to the fire goes without saying, but *I*
wanted more, and to become actual
   Woman. Who cares if the passage is haunted

Territory? Aren't all girlhoods that of a kind?
   Our desires exceed the Human project, in the end, throws
One on all fours, to the floor,
   Pour into me. An illish light pours into the perfect animal,
Makes wings. I am your last fallen angel.

TERROTICA

You think that Gender is true.

*

   That the only Way thru is you, tho I be like Mist tomorrow.
Other than grammar, the *Function* of Gender is treatment:
   how to Act; Be so Acted upon; how to Treat; how to Treat them; who Attract;
Tactical decisions; Be so 'Tracted to; the Drama of the Family,
   the Bother of the Mutable Sexed Body, then Categorizing said Bodies,
their latitude among Society, their welcome along Strata, Right
or Wrong voice (*hollering, versus the neon shrill of a scream*)
   Carnal sentiments, and other Errata. The Soul *does* care, about the Gender,
     But prefers one's Character (as in one's Purpose), which is where I've been.
My Soul is Coolly Feminine, and Bending necks of violets in flash wind.

SPIRAL, SURROUNDED BY SPOILED ACCORD (*OR, LATER UNIVERSE*)

—after diagnosis

What I have done is created
History, exquisite manuscripts
   with angering blame.

What I have done is created

   manuscripts

in pity of me

   culpable

my Spain loneliness

   exquisite

in pity of me

   misery

What I have done is created

   manuscripts

berserk with anger

   culpable

berserk with anger

   history

What I have done is created

   misery

Do I know myself?

   manuscripts

Do I know myself?

   history

What I have done is created

   culpable

Blame, a spoilt milk

   manuscripts

A spoilt romance

   misery

What I have done is created

   culpable

  Blame angered with berserk
Manuscripts exquisiting history.
   What's created is done. What have I?

AN ELEGY

after Melvin Dixon's "Heartbeats"

The stubbornness of me always healant & fine.
The fore-ongoingness of me rhymed with linger,
Longer, Iron. Face graces itself (*"sweet heart"*) despite a brutal,
Physical harangue: so is the problem that I changed
And didn't scar? (*"Don't stop."*) That I be now
Subdued as sphinxes go; my spine yet a donnée of fire
That, like fire, gains from all its converts to char.
Such slim chance then, in the end, I'd be hopeless
& penny; that I'd be like a gazelle giving up its long neck
To the dark Sahara. But I am leaping yet, and easy,
As when water breaks from the sky, however rare,
Giving up its awesome, rainy tinuance, both will
& miracle, over to some dirt, and I am neither stubborn
Dirt left to die: I, like dirt, do not die. I survive. I rain.
And I *Melvin-Dixon* my life. *"Heartbeats." "Work out."*
"Call home." The Sahara is greening again. The lions
May once again stalk Babylon. The clean incredible
Reality, whatever happens, I will have to last it out,
My past (*simple pain*) with all pasts (*honest pain*) as after
My futures, which is rain come without Jupiter this time,
That vein of cruelty gone white and beautifully
Against sumpter night. *"Heart beats." "Get mad." "Fatigue."*
I didn't deserve Half as much has happened to me, tho I
Reserve their trouble, the knowledge therein; reserve
The *bourgie,* chronic unavailability to my running
Sorrows, my Happiness demands—Them I'm also
Served; am ergo light; am ergo light; heat; sense, reborn.
I think I will keep this idea: Sense.
Whether we would Die at the sprawn of pain's glutty
Sensation; whether we would delay, not pain, but its hot,

Joveous, greedy knowledge; whether we'd become
Citizens all afled of pain, save that anxiety it should return
("*No air*"); whether simply surpass pain, staunch it, or would
Have it abated ("*No air*") to nourish later. I mean, to drink
Pains in as to have recorded one's life lived. "*Breathe in.*" "*Breathe out.*"
Yes. Ergo love. Ergo death (*All Doubts, Stop Haunting*). Ergo art.

BLACK HOLE (*OR, TOTAL ECLIPSE 2024*)

Not every black bird is blackbird, Wally, Wallace Stevens, some can be starlings, be crow,
  and
be ravens' weird un*kind*nesses smack
  wild to the sky, now why call it that? those nouns' collective? like a surname? why explain it
in the negative? *un*kindness? what it mean? just
  —as—

not every winds' pairings spring alarum, some La Sirene, others *Salomé,* for any company,
  argonaut
or friend or foe,
  distinctions they *do* matter (*mediocrity ain't it*) specific words matter (*black mediocrity ain't
    it*)
as not every black is black, tho I be black
  bird singing in the brisk, shifty, grayish, might-pour weather today (*not every black need be
excellent*) weather
  in New Orleans is windy brisk, versus *madd brick,* so you see I get it, everything can't
    change,
hasn't,
or slip, just as not everyone is artist and what even *is a* "creative"? artisan, laborer or surgeon
you mean?——but *care* remember the heart (*it is time again, we millennials all, to do*

  Our work) the heart in all totality, of our galaxy? yes? (*Werk*) it is in Total Eclipse,
the event, right now, 12 som'n p.m., *exactly,* April 8, 2024, so that I'm *captive* (*but not slave*) to
  it,
  my femme gaze,
less eros than in holy attitudes, be pulled up, at, and into,
——for gazes *penetrate*——

My silly mortal Brown eyes, look up at its majestic (*if scarer or rarer*), corona'd majesty,
   chilly
eclipse, what appears to me now (*behind Warby Parker glasses*) the deepest,
   O! the Blackest of, Wet
Gorgeous
   origin, Black
Hole.

   *

Wayback. A boy looks Down a Manhole's Hole to see what work some shadows do.

THE MAKING OF THE COMPLETE LOVER

—Walt Whitman

I.

Because at least You loved always Your Mind,
Time spent in Jussive tense with it, You loved Yourself, despite—
   Despite when it was Back when You could've easily collapsed . . .
then You could think *Love it* and *Have*
   Your Soul's prize. I, again,
Stood out & doused the air coppery.
   Repeat to the mirror, in Heart's tempo: *You I love completely.*

2. *Did I always know could Love like that? Love my Body?*

   All but collided. But once I conceded I *be*
my Soul-goings, a Soul being that distance sits between Existences
   and the Overall perfection, the Damn Life fled right out
so that The Gladder Hour come thru.
   Refuse stress. Sipping soda, think, *Choose Happiness.*
When it was You *weren't* Your Body & Hated &
   At least Doubted Yourself,
You chose stress. Being that You were convicted to the Lie
   that rolled Headaches down Your spine,
Your Body's so-called Insufficiencies red-marked, You choose no Happiness.
   So, the answer is No.

3. *Should I believe that?*

—Ergo, We are Gorgeous largely for forgoing such Tarny ignorance, for
-getting Love's presence,
   which a Body requires. You require spoken intent. That Bitch
to be Reckoned with, tested, lewdly
   Here, who think she's worthy, Lord, Free, & yet grounded: She was me, she believes it.

She has assumed the agency requisite to Choose
  thyself, and truly Be Responsible for it.
It's just that I was sick & tired of always being sick & tired, you know?
  You know how it is . . .

4. *How it went?*

It took ten or so gross, weird years at least; it took twenty,
    and tears—Mirror, Shade, Shadow, & Light
work & Head Voices. It took sobbing tears. Carework.
    For real life, I supposed it could be true
To enjoy it and Look as if I did. *Have grace.*
    For me, dysphoria was in my Body *literal;* it punctuated; it wrote
Criticism in my blood. At any reflected surface, any trace,
    for years I avoided them but when I couldn't
I despised my face.

3.

  But now, delight in it. Cherish it, Cherish it,
Sweet confrontation, let me tell You how—

4. (On Remembering the Body)

  —dismembering, limb by limb, such Patient surgery, my Body
as to remember—rhyme by rhyme—my Body well, & whole,
    I became a Mystery,
a tried-and-true Drama of the Trauma I inherited from a Straightened World,
    ever Stridently striving but Failing their Queues.
Yet I, by and by, tipsy, jubilant, sibilant I found myself more actually
    in a kind of Mental Passion, then such Play, then such Paradigm
Would shoo away the Generation's dread, if still not cure Pain,
    the dreaded Shames, if not yet Anxiety; provoke
& So approach (*versus Vanity*) truest Beauty, which is won in the Mind.

5. *What is the name of this Spell?*

Continued Ritual of the Boy Isis; or Astraea's Return;
   Or that Miracle Play; or the Little Decade
of Increasingly More Useful, Tender Smiles; or Initiation;
   Or the New Evangelism, with Her Lucid Veil, Star
Overhead & Psychic Wings, Self-Actualizing:
   Decade in which each summer blazed with a deliberate,
discriminant-to-each-body-part's
   Nudity, as the intent *was* to be seen,
That would truly release me to my goal, which was to Obsess
   Less compulsively everyone's gazes, not to believe
the Lie my Mind assumed in their eyes each time:
   They hate me, have they hated me, don't desire, they hate me—

6. *And was that wrong?*

—Exactly that I had heretofore felt, always, cloaked in Wrongfeeling,
   I ordered these steps, which are not Wrong. *Find honor.* I didn't know
I could be a Woman, *if* I should, *if* I should ask permission,
   Until I was a Woman, & exactly what's at issue
With adding more Women?

7. (On Remembering the Body)

   And so I dressed each hated part
of my Body deliberately, to let it ride in the male & female gazes.
   Evidently, You will assume why.
Evidently, You almost need not ask at all.
   But You will try as well this Ritual, anyway,
And assume wider: *We go toward Ourselves*
   thru the Body. We are any of us good for the Soul.
Now Remember: First Legs (*I wore shorts*), then Waist (*crop tops*),
   then Ass (*I wore skinnies*), then Hips (*et al.*)—

8. *Each item?*

   By item. If I didn't want anyone seeing it, want having it,
I made them see it, claimed it, and I didn't collapse. And I made me grieve
   the certain discomforts with myself
what might've only ever been in my Mind, sutured there by an Insidious World,
And slowly over time—I made me grieve my death.
   Withstand it, I said. Stay Easy: it became my mantra,
For all future comforts started off an itch, a wound, You would either Scratch out
   or Tear it further in or Pass thru. Pass thru. The Body,
until it is Treated in Concert, in Coherence, with its Society, is not
   a Complete Thing. It creeps on old hinges, forced into
the Burning Closet. It
fringes, yet requires—

9. *Why lie?*

   (*Everything lies.*) Then Appendages,
then Arms (*I wore wifebeaters*), my Back (*I wore nothing*), & Hips again,
   then finally came Face, and it was a while
 Till its feminine Eyes would rise up,
   Like hopeful flags. If it's a lie to say *You're beautiful,* dutifully in the mirror,
Banally, as while brushing Your teeth,
   Repeating each day, each Day falling off the Good Bough like rose petals—
If it's a lie to ritualize my gladdest
   Responsibility, to Heal by *Speaking to Thine Brain* directly,
then it's a lie supplies Fate,
   Not Conspiracy. Makes of a penultimate Self her ultimate,
 who I'll just call *The Person*—

10. *Why lie?*

   Always Choose in The Person, where Power lies and is invented.
Forgive into Your face. *Have solidarity.* Make
   remind Yourself You *are* a liberal claim, Precious Body,
with Huge prerogative—

I did.

And, ridiculously, I didn't die. You won't die. I *thrill* where was a thorn, just to be alive & mine.
  You can, too.

No more Gods. No more Slaves. *We change.*

  And I am suddenly a Species sublime. See? Now the Sun also rises,

Now the Mississippi becomes the Nile wildly roaming, Bold again, and for thee.

VICTIM

—Judges 19

My life came due to natural causes, so I'm not sorry I changed.
Beauty is changes. And, Beauty will save the World! I am the Prize of the Slaughter,
Portion of a Final Covenant with the Wandering Herd, or I am not
The Lamb but yet in his Blood; the Bloodwife, the Lamb's Bride, the Gotten-To,
& Already Herself; yet in his Blood is ambition & I'm sorry it changed
& nevermind the Blood creates not Two Snakes' anti-venom, quietly
(The one snake's Slavery) by science of the antibody (the next snake's Freedom),
But hardly one Relation. I'm sorry you changed. And I am sorry for my anger,
All its given changes, my zealous, roaming chill & so I go now garish,
If extramundane later, 'til finally the Blood do Cools like the Soul reaches the navel.
I'm sorry you're sorry I changed. So, this is why my Soul's been so so
Angry? But I am not sorry for such danger, of a Will's tour thru passion:
   rather, that I was angry,
Rather that I recognized my Care or my Dignity had been compromised,
Hit so in the jaw, Denied, Freeborn, & since living Trans, I'm not sorry.
I'm not sorry I changed. Time's the rudest healer. Everyone wants make me over.
Time don't heel. But I have had enough weeping. On this day you will ask me
Each & proper use of and please say all my names. I went everywhere
The people could see me. (I'm sorry I swear.) I went all evening. I was like one Mouth
Now is cupping another, I screamed my kiss out, thru any Dive's door, Poor
Boys, across tracks, to nearly anyone, begging, seducing my song, please, let me belong.
"A King is dead!" I sang, but the Brave Ruler never dies. Long live the Coup of Her Majesty.
Gender in the World is in heaty English crisis, but sorry no—all is not Wrong in the world.
The years are moving serif. The Way to the Story ain't long. Still, we do not know
What our nature permits us to be, And strange how the fire is still burning. But I was saying,
if Gender had survived in English, we wouldn't be here, all of us 'Mankind,'
all of us or, perhaps, just you, now, reader, less decapitated as mind-collapsed,
At the fact of my face appointed in oil, the length of this Book's Obsession;
We wouldn't be sick, not just my waist's ever dis- & re-
Appearing invitation, but so too my Voice's, or how I afford even that Blackest creature,

The Female, lovely case for the word, "Woman," that precious title, "Person," again.
But don't I deserve such honors, too? I weep. I play the Wounded all too well, like a Gypsy
In America, and still I offend. Except that some Voice exceptionalized me, I sustain.
I have been like an Oyster, have Born the Waters, have delivered the Pearl & the Fish.
And I have only looked like that Biblical concubine thrown to the Levite's door's threshold,
After she was given to a full night of rape, for which she is cut up twelve times for the twelve
Tribes of Israel, or the twelve Keys of the Zodiac, an Act which inaugurates a kid war,
For there are concubines no more. We are today, all of us, Better persons. We walk
Beyond our doors, slapping the faces of our enemies but by our Beauty's power.
  Some Beauties Have no soul:
a bartender spoke this, once, direct into each eye. It wasn't advice. It was a wet
Wish dangled at me, but turned out inconclusive. My Soul, if Souls immortal endure due
Changes, kept changing for the damages it politely received, what suffering is, all to Touch
At another Soul pure, which is why we're Born, to be both Self- & otherwise possessed,
That is why transform. Yea! that I am the Victim, Tribute of the Slaughter, giddy Virgin
Bride & the Lamb, in whose Blood, anticipates. Death is the Maker of Origins.
You will read no lyric more so spell be done. You will shut me up. Even you weary of the joke.
You will put me down now, a Victim, into the Altar's fire, so I wind up uttered as Smoke.

An ancient source for trans forebears might, since stable notions of identity qua race, gender & sexuality are largely modern fixations, always disappoint. Yet antecedents (epicene masques, twice-borns, two-spirits, the twins, &c) do exist, in both mortal and divine, tolerated and policed, positive and negative forms, a whole stratosphere of existence. Here we recall Pliny's words: "There are beings that unite the two sexes, we call them hermaphrodites; they used to be called androgynous, and they were looked upon as monsters. Today they delight in the delights of '*libertineity*,'" which is to say the delights of a future, next, liberated world.

Not only do I, in "Steal Away," allude to the Negro spiritual of the same name, a song which preserves mystery on its own, but I also paraphrase Seneca writing, in *Quaestiones Naturales VII*, his instruction "There are holy things that are not communicated all at once: Eleusis always keeps something back to show those who come again." I would offer New Orleans as a modern-day Eleusis, appropriate for the New World.

The series "The Punishment of Tiresias" and "Auspices" concern the mythic elder figure Tiresias, who was much enjoyed across the Greek archaic and antique periods. He was a Seer or Augur who, by various accounts, and for various reasons (including being born so) had said abilities, and so is famously consulted to his doom by Oedipus in *Oedipus Rex*. It's an early tale in which an older, praised-for-his-wise-ways man, forever mobile, strikes with his rod two snakes copulating, and whose punishment, by the Goddess of the Hearth, Hera, no less, is to be a woman, and for several years. In my version, during such period he conceives a daughter called Manto.

In one of the Tiresiad poems, the archaic fragment is from *Clytemnestra*.

The poem "2019," its title notably referring to the last year prior to the COVID pandemic outbreak, commemorated one hundred years since 1919, a year of considerable global, postwar unrest and also, in the United States, the year of the Red Summer, which saw more than three dozen race riots pepper the nation. Vigilante or police violence resulted in hundreds of Black casualties, including the lynching of Mr. William Brown. Although we're apparently given to an adamantly progressive interpretation of history—an eventual "bend toward justice"—it's just as useful, I think, to consider regression, or how little, in fact, has changed.

I wrote the the poem "2019" after writing another one that celebrated Black, queer pleasure had been declined for publication by the Academy of American Poets. So, I wrote "2019" in a kind of angry reflection, assured that Black Death would, instead, be deemed publishable. You should read the poem as if it is addressed to a "Sir," or those towering white powers that decide American publishing.

"Beautiful Bottom, Beautiful Shame" is a title I borrowed from Kathryn Bond Stockton's book of the same name.

"Hymn" recalls the time at the turn of the last century when hymns were still a prominent Christian genre. This period was also the dawn of a largely female-organized Temperance movement, soon to bleed into the movement for woman suffrage outright. Emily Hackett, a fierce campaigner for these movements, once remarked: "It is easy to conquer a man if you only know how. I wish you could see me talking to some of these saloon men that I would never have spoken to before. I employ my sweetest accents. I exhaust all the arguments I am possessed of. I look into their eyes and grow pathetic. I shed tears and I joke with them but all in terrible earnest. And they surrender."

A function of racism, said Toni Morrison, distracts us not just from our lives' work, but the natural world as well; distraction from either body expires that body, eventually. So this must cycle needs be killed at the root. My admiration goes to the work of Rue Mapp—founder of Outdoor Afro, which celebrates Black connections and leadership in nature—if especially for her language, some of which inspired the poem. Readers might also recognize lyrics from a younger Kanye West, a lyric from his 2005 song "Touch the Sky" is repeated, slightly altered, in the poem.

I first arrived in Palestine, contemplated in the long poem "Toward a Tall Lyric for Palestine (*Or, The Harder Thinking*)," through the Jordan Corridor, with the Palestine Festival of Literature in 2016, accompanied by exemplaries such as J. M. Coetzee, Saidiya Hartman, and others. Though Hartman, the only other Black American on the caravan, passed thru easily, I was barred for an hour at the first checkpoint with some others, all of them Arab travelers. How come? Also, where I mention "doubler consciousness" I refer to W. E. B. DuBois's theory of Black persons' double consciousness, which keeps divided interests between Blackness and what he called "Americanness" (or whiteness) ever within the confines of Black life. Can there be more?

Careful readers will notice "Improvising on an Early Theme (*Or, One Country*)" was first published in *Boy with Thorn*, but they will also find new emphasis.

In "Prodigy, Versus Prodigy" we do well to remember a "prodigy is a phenomenon," or so says Ralph Evêque, "an out of the ordinary incident caused, according to the Romans, by a divine action intended to reveal an imminent rupture of the Pax deorum, the concord between men and gods." In Rome, differently than in earlier civilizations such as the Babylonian, Greek, or Egyptian, "every portion had to be absolutely male or female," and thus intersexed persons of any or various degree meant grave news. It required swift action. Yet today "prodigy" arrives to our ear entirely differently, as a marvel.

My two poems "*Boy* Coming Out *Gay* Going Far to *Lady* Way to *Queer*" and "*Girl* Going *Boy* Coming Back to *Girl* Going *Woman*," which are heavily hyphenated, borrow language, a kind of taxonomic impulse, found in *The Casta Paintings*, with thanks to Natasha Trethewey for bringing this source to my attention, and Carl Phillips, who is also mentioned in the other poem. *The Casta Paintings* describes a colonial caste or lineage system that desired, through the combined efforts of pseudoscience, folk knowledge, and aesthetics, to create a schematics for returning the various mixed & other nonwhite races *back* to a white, pure, "unstained" ideal; it became the subject of many paintings and literary works. As I use it, or, better said, apply the logic, I'm considering gender in a similar, if its own, paradigm, as within today's understanding of a spectrum in a similar variety as shown, with regard to race, in *The Casta Paintings*—well realizing, however, the sure pitfalls of such a logical application with regard to spectral scope, gender, or race. About our gender paradigms, this much it at least true: there can never be just one notion, one static idea of just two genders in a binary, again; but let nuance exist.

Michael Rea writes in his essay "Gender as a Divine Attribute," "By virtue of the relationship between masculinity and maleness, this pattern might seem to suggest that males bear the image of God to a greater degree than females, that they are more fit to represent God, and that whatever traits contribute to making someone masculine are somehow more divine than whatever traits contribute to making someone feminine." So many traditionalists have thought; so many feminists have objected. I would place agree with the latter.

"Two Seconds the Slave (*Or, Carnival Baby*)" references Steve McQueen's film *12 Years a Slave*, which documents, from his written account, the capture of Solomon Northup, a man abducted from New York and shipped to New Orleans (a major internal port of slavery within the nation) to his loneliness, his bondage. But this poem also, surprisingly, breaks out & references a particular phenomenon seen among those who are, insultingly somehow, called "transmedicalists" or, simply, trans people. According to a paper by Brian A. Rood & others in the periodical *Transgender Health,* trans rejection "could happen anytime when out in public spaces or when there is the potential to meet new people" or in the Home. This is the phenomenon of trans persons in situations which engender solicitation by potential romantic advance, immediately presuppose (because of acute, past experiences) their rejection on the basis of their trans identity, then, when advances are, in fact, taken back, or turn bullyish if accusatory, the solicitation is retracted so that trans rejection is realized. "Expecting rejection," the article goes on, "is described . . . as a form of felt stigma, which is understood as an individual's knowledge of society's stance toward nonmajority individuals, and expectations regarding the likelihood of stigma being enacted in a given situation as a result of having a minority status, for example, for sexual and gender minority individuals." This stigma is compounded for individuals with dual minority status, i.e., trans persons who are Black or persons of color (compounded by weight or attractiveness maybe?) or i.e., trans queer persons, i.e., me.

Just as well, according to a medical paper by André Hajek, Katharina Grupp & others, the term "trans loneliness," used in the poem "Trans Loneliness," refers to "high prevalence rates of loneliness and social isolation . . . shown among transgender and gender diverse people." Indeed, as Carl Jung reminds us, "Loneliness does not come from having no people about one, but from being unable to communicate the things that seem important to oneself, or from holding certain views which others find inadmissible." This sonnet, written to a pioneer trans woman, if not all Black trans women, incorporates the pharmaceutical names some of our hormonal regimens use. Where the single quotation marks appear, I mean to put pressure on and reveal some ways figurative language is excused, and where it's refused too often with regard to "woman." This is a striking narrow-mindedness given it wasn't so many decades ago only the pronoun "he," and the term "Man," was deployed in reference to any crowd of mixed or unknown gender, and could even generally apply to and represent all of humanity, as how Oscar Wilde meant when he said, "Disobedience, in the eyes of any one who has read history, is man's original virtue." He continues: "It is through disobedience that progress has been made, through disobedience and through rebellion."

The being named in the title of "Hermaphrodite! (*Or, Sacred Paeon*)" is divine Hermaphroditus, born of two godly parents. So one wonders at the slight and injury this figure has received throughout history. And one also wonders, when Slick Rick, Dr. Dre, Nas, Lil Wayne, Missy Elliott, Cam'ron, Dwayne Johnson or The Rock, Cassidy, Meek Mill, and counting, if when they used the term, often pejoratively & seldom correctly, "hermaphrodite" in their young genre, did they remember the place of distinction such trans bodies played in our ancient knowledge, prior to the overcorrecting mandate of white Christendom? Such was recorded in Eusebius's *The Life of Constantine* when he wrote, "And inasmuch as the Egyptians, especially those of Alexandria, had been accustomed to honor their river god [that is, the Arrival of Hapi, portrayed androgynously with protruded breasts through a priesthood composed of hermaphrodites, a further law was passed [by Constantine] commanding the extermination of the whole class as vicious, that no one might thenceforward be found tainted with the like impurity?" I wonder?

Androgyny of any kind, so says scholar Maria Grazia Lancellotti, evokes "a fierceness of disposition beyond control, lust made furious," one such "derived from both sexes." This disposition is certainly recalled in Hermaphroditos and the Phrygian Agdistis, while that lust might be explained as a callback to Aristophanes's original model for humanity in his creation story on the origin of love. In it, he posits all humans began as circular androgynies of the male and female, before Zeus, fearing humans would usurp his power, sent lightning to split humanity up in such a way that formed "men" and "women," the two in eager search of her "other half," or his "soulmate," and their "holistic circle."

"At Voodoo Lounge" recounts a true story. I quote the essay "Use of the Erotic" by Audre Lorde, also referenced later in a poem bearing the same title. "You will find you have fallen in love with your own *vision*," Audre Lorde also said, "which you may never have realized you had. And you will lose some friends and lovers, and realize you don't miss them. And new ones will find you and cherish you. And at last you'll know with surpassing certainty that only one thing is more frightening than speaking your truth. And that is not speaking."

Theory of sexual inversion arrived in the late nineteenth century, where the invert "was believed to be an inborn reversal of gender traits: male inverts were, to a greater or lesser degree, inclined to traditionally *female* pursuits and dress" and vice versa for female inverts. Thru correctly reinscribing the more "appropriate" gendered embodiments upon the invert's body, the homosexual would experience a broader society that could better accept them—a still improbable prospect that by the Turn of the Millennium's Born-This-Way (that is, Born Gay) mentality had been differently absorbed, sluggishly accepted.

One swan worth keeping in mind while reading "The Vague Year (*Or, At the End of the World My Long Psychosis Began*)" is William Dorsey Swann, considered by many a pioneer of the trans movement. Although this designation might've been made too soon, since again no such identifiable, stable identity category as "trans" could've existed at that time, one cannot help but admire Swann, who knew and fashioned herself as a woman just years after the emancipation of the slave. At least the law authority saw and were convinced enuf of the scandal gender plays to have warranted repeated arrests on the charges of "vagrancy." Such a charge often returned the relatively recently freed person back to the farm or plantation as punishment. She, with her peers, kept on; they threw what were known as "Drag Balls," their name referring to the popular style of music, ragtime, made famous by Scott Joplin; it is also the earliest, immediately relevant usage of the term "drag" in American culture. Consider some lyrics of "The Ragtime Dance": "Let me see you do the 'ragtime dance' / Turn left and do the 'Cake-walk prance' / Turn the other way and do the 'Slow Drag' / Now take your lady to the world's fair and do the 'ragtime dance.'"

In "All Good Things Will Be Added unto You (*Or, The Epiphany*)" I have in mind the Negro spiritual sung beautifully by Phylicia Rashad with the Morehouse & Spelman Colleges' choirs on one relatively rare episode of the understandably retired comedy *The Cosby Show*. The reader will also note that, as a result of violence seen against my person while transitioning—more than ten occasions when cis persons have attacked or struck me—I now live with PTSD after a true psychiatric ordeal where sometimes I was rendered mute and catatonic. I am gratefully able today, after much determination, to snatch back my mind. Importantly, I've survived.

For "You Would Be Christ," see my earlier poem "You Are Not Christ." The poem, especially by the second stanza, is spoken from the perspective of Peter, whose name means rock.

Speaking to the Slave Narrative Collection of the Federal Writers' Project, a New Deal program, one formerly enslaved person had to say: "Slavery was a bad thing," said Patsy Mitchner, of life after Emancipation in Raleigh, North Carolina. "And freedom, of the kind we got with nothing to live on, was bad. Two snakes full of poison. One lying with his head pointing north, the other with his head pointing south. Their names were slavery and freedom. The snake called slavery lay with his head pointed south, and the snake called freedom lay with his head pointed north. Both," she relayed, "bit the [Black person], and they were both bad."

In an 1858 article, "The Coup d'Etat in New-Orleans," published in *The New York Times,* the author explains, "New-Orleans is, unquestionably, the most un-American city in our whole Confederacy. The French and Spanish population, though less than the Anglo-Saxon in point of numbers, do, nevertheless, give the dominant tone to the morals of the people. They form, too, the permanent population of the city, for the emigrants from the Northern States are mostly absorbed by their business pursuits, and take but little interest in local politics," though the author denies the powerful effect African and enslaved cultures wrote across the city and region, too. Nearly two hundred years later, though, New Orleans remains that cagey city, overwhelmed and consumed, mischaracterized and continued by competing Northern, Anglo or "all-American," or even European cultures who would possess it, descending by way of their post-Katrina coups, yet won't totally, definitively, know or call the city all their own. They ain't *from* here, as we say. It is a tension, the author notes, that reprises itself ever in society's many notions of identity. "New Orleans is often called the northernmost Caribbean city," said *The Boston Globe,* in another article published in 1997. "A. J. Liebling once described it as a cross between Port-au-Prince and Paterson, N.J., with a culture not unlike that of Genoa, Marseilles, Beirut, or Egyptian Alexandria. . . . Contrary to popular usage outside New Orleans, the word 'creole' there has nothing to do with race or racial mixtures." Oh, really? "It simply means native-born."

Acknowledgments

My thanks to my editor, John Freeman, and everyone at Knopf; and to my agents, Leslie Shipman of the Shipman speakers' agency and Jin Auh of the Wylie Agency. With regard to friends, I am much indebted for their patience and help over these last years: Devan Shimoyama, Camonghne Felix, Jonathan Dunn, Yona Harvey; my extended family, Terrance Hayes, Natalie Diaz, Ocean Vuong, Safiya Sinclair, Haley Josephs, the orisha, and, in a strange way, even those inhabitants of the Abandoned Base of New Orleans, especially Josh and Tracey; and to Zoe. All my sustained friendships, I write with an appreciation of you.

Some of these poems have appeared, if in much different form, in *Poetry; Poet Lore; Literary Hub; The New Republic;* thru the Academy of American Poets; *The Scores,* a journal of the United Kingdom; *Cassius;* and other journals.

This book honors the memory of too many Black trans women, gone too soon, and to queer and trans others who are yet alive!

A NOTE ABOUT THE AUTHOR

Rickey Laurentiis was born in New Orleans, Louisiana, to care. She is the recipient of many awards, some of the most recent being the Whiting Award, the Ruth Lilly and Lannan Fellowships, and an inaugural fellowship from the Center for African American Poetry & Poetics. In 2022, she was named a Living Legend by the Martha P. Johnson Institute for Black Transgender People. Their first book, *Boy with Thorn*, won the Cave Canem and Levis Reading Prizes. They can be accessed at rickeylaurentiis.com.

A NOTE ON THE TYPE

This book was set in Fournier, a typeface named for Pierre-Simon Fournier le Jeune (1712–1768), a celebrated French type designer. Coming from a family of typefounders, Fournier was an extraordinarily prolific designer of typefaces and typographic ornaments. He was also the author of the important *Manuel typographique* (1764–1766), in which he attempted to work out a system standardizing type measurement in points, a system that is still in use internationally. Fournier's type is considered transitional in that it drew its inspiration from the old style yet was ingeniously innovational, providing for an elegant, legible appearance. In 1925 his type was revived by the Monotype Corporation of London.

Composed by North Market Street Graphics
Lancaster, Pennsylvania

Book design by Pei Loi Koay

A NOTE ABOUT THE AUTHOR

Rickey Laurentiis was born in New Orleans, Louisiana, to care. She is the recipient of many awards, some of the most recent being the Whiting Award, the Ruth Lilly and Lannan Fellowships, and an inaugural fellowship from the Center for African American Poetry & Poetics. In 2022, she was named a Living Legend by the Martha P. Johnson Institute for Black Transgender People. Their first book, *Boy with Thorn*, won the Cave Canem and Levis Reading Prizes. They can be accessed at rickeylaurentiis.com.

A NOTE ON THE TYPE

This book was set in Fournier, a typeface named for Pierre-Simon Fournier le Jeune (1712–1768), a celebrated French type designer. Coming from a family of typefounders, Fournier was an extraordinarily prolific designer of typefaces and typographic ornaments. He was also the author of the important *Manuel typographique* (1764–1766), in which he attempted to work out a system standardizing type measurement in points, a system that is still in use internationally. Fournier's type is considered transitional in that it drew its inspiration from the old style yet was ingeniously innovational, providing for an elegant, legible appearance. In 1925 his type was revived by the Monotype Corporation of London.

Composed by North Market Street Graphics
Lancaster, Pennsylvania

Book design by Pei Loi Koay